CALLING

Thoughts on England,
the English and Englishness

Colin Joyce

Translated by
Hiroyuki Morita

NHK Publishing

LONDON CALLING
Thoughts on England, the English and Englishness

Copyright © 2014 by Colin Joyce & Hiroyuki Morita
ISBN 978-4-14-035125-3 C0082
All rights reserved.
Published in Japan by NHK Publishing, Inc. (NHK Shuppan)

No part of this book may be used or reproduced in any manner whatsoever without written permission, except in the case of brief quotations embodied in critical articles and reviews.

For information:
NHK Publishing, Inc. (NHK Shuppan)
41-1 Udagawa-cho, Shibuya, Tokyo, 150-8081, Japan
http://www.nhk-book.co.jp

Printed in Japan

Book Design by Takeshi Hatanaka
Proofreading by Yoko Otsuka
DTP by Dolphin

LONDON CALLING

Thoughts on England,
the English and Englishness

CONTENTS

Preface	7
1 English People Are Nice	13
2 The Little Jar of Englishness	18
3 My Unloved Home County	23
4 The Art of Purchasing	28
5 Journeying to Frustration	33
6 Pride and Pearl Buttons	39
7 The London Slang Dictionary	44
8 A Secret, Sometimes Funny Language	52
9 The National Obsession	57
10 How to Buy a Pint of Beer	63
11 A Song for England	69

12 London's "Other" Waterway 75

13 Talking About Weather 81

14 The Accidental Gardener 87

15 A Peculiarly British Alien 92

日本語訳

はじめに 100

1 イギリス人は親切だ 105

2 イギリスらしさが詰まった小瓶 109

3 愛されないぼくの故郷 113

4 イギリス式住宅購入術 117

5 欲求不満への旅 121

CONTENTS

6 真珠のボタンは、誇りのボタン　　　125

7 ロンドン・スラング小辞典　　　129

8 ときどきおかしな、秘密の言葉　　　136

9 国民的強迫観念　　　140

10 1パイントのビールの買い方　　　145

11 イングランドの歌　　　150

12 ロンドンの「もうひとつ」の水路　　　155

13 天気の話をする　　　159

14 偶然の庭師　　　163

15 奇妙にイギリス人らしいエイリアン　　　167

Preface

It's a strange thing to live overseas for a long time. I left England when I was still in my early twenties and only returned in 2010, having spent the best part of two decades abroad in Japan and the US.

I visited England a lot during that time, but living away from it for that length of time made me a bit of a stranger in my own country. Or at least it made me a bit different from most of my countrymen.

Curiously, the further away I was from England the more important my "Englishness" became. People would introduce me by saying, "This is Colin. He's from England." Quite often, people would ask me to explain something about England or the English way of doing things. This might be just a casual question from a friend, but sometimes I was asked to propound "as a British journalist" and my words would be published.

Sometimes I wondered if I was still really English at all. I noticed, for example, that I knew the city of Tokyo like the back of my hand. I had crossed it on foot, by bicycle and by train, investigating its every corner. With London, meanwhile, there were whole swathes I had never visited. I had travelled widely in Japan, but had not very often ventured beyond the south-east of England in my own country.

I wondered too if I had changed culturally. I knew what I wasn't. I wasn't Japanese (despite more than a decade living happily there) and I wasn't American (despite three years there). I like to think my experiences of living overseas had broadened my horizons and made my life more interesting. But I also felt I lost a certain reassurance by becoming a bit less English. So what was I?

My attitude towards England veered between highly patriotic and highly critical. I would read something in a newspaper or hear a story from a friend and it would have a big effect on me, one way or the other. I think it's because I was hearing it in isolation from the broader experience of living in Britain. A political scandal would sicken me, because I would not be aware that many British politicians also do their jobs quietly and diligently. Or I would hear of a brilliant new comedy and see it as evidence of our great cultural richness, because I wasn't flicking through channels in Britain and seeing how much dross was now on display ("reality" TV, cooking programmes, silly "talent" shows etc.)

It is sometimes said that expats retain an image of their country that is frozen in time on the day they left. That wasn't quite true for me, but Britain did seem to be changing faster than I could follow. I would return home after a year's absence and find things subtly but unsettlingly different.

Finally, I decided that the solution was to return to Britain and to get to grips with this half-alien, half-familiar place. I had set out overseas as a young man because I wanted to learn a foreign language and experience other places. Now, I decided I was ready for the "new" experience of learning about my own country.

The essays in this book were originally published in NHK's *Radio Eikawa*. They cover a period of three years, starting with my arrival back in Britain a bit disorientated. I see it as a bit of a journey, as I was gradually getting used to being back even as I was filing these pieces once a month. Sometimes, I tried to write about what I thought readers would be most interested in. Sometimes, I dared to write about what I was most interested in. Other times I just wrote about what was preoccupying me at the time (such as our lousy trains) because I felt it would give an immediate sense of what it was like to be in Britain.

Many people helped me in my work. In particular, Namiko Okumura has been patient and

PREFACE

encouraging when I was writing these pieces; I was lucky to work with someone who knows Britain very well but let me write about it from my perspective. Takeshi Nakano has been supportive. Hiroyuki Morita, as always, is a sensitive translator who has had to tolerate me "peering over his shoulder" in a way that most translators never have to with authors.

Some people ask me why the columns and this book are titled *London Calling* even though I don't live in London. The BBC used to begin its broadcasts on the World Service with those words and—though I don't claim to be the official voice of Britain in the way the BBC can—I liked the idea that I was, in a way, sending out a message from Britain to beyond. There is also a pop song I am rather fond of called "London Calling" by The Clash. I liked the symmetry that my previous essay collection (*An Englishman in N.Y.*) also derives its title from a pop song (this one by Sting).

Lastly, there is a personal meaning to the title *London Calling*. My desire to go back to England nagged at me most of the time I was away, however much I was enjoying my life. In that sense, I always felt my country was calling me.

1

English People Are Nice

Shortly after I arrived back in England I suffered a small but annoying injury. I pulled a leg muscle quite badly playing football and had to be carried off the field by my team-mates. It was terrible timing as a friend was arriving from New York the next day and we had a busy week of sightseeing planned — and now I could barely walk a few hundred yards.

I hoped the injury would miraculously improve overnight, but in fact it was stiffer and sorer after sleeping. I knew it wasn't a serious injury and it would heal naturally but I felt incredibly unlucky.

Several months on, however, I actually feel it was a *lucky* accident. Yes, it was a major inconvenience during my friend's visit but it was also a wonderful way to be reacquainted with my countrymen, the English. The reason is that suddenly everybody was really nice to me. Incredibly nice, I would say.

I didn't generally think of the English as particularly nice. I have met a lot of unpleasant ones over the years, partly because I grew up in a town famous for not being particularly friendly or polite. In the years I lived in Japan I couldn't help but notice how much more polite the Japanese were than the English. And in the US I found people open and friendly in a way that I never found the English to be. The longer I was away the more negatively I came to think of the English and, to be honest, I wasn't entirely looking forward to living among them again.

But that changed with the accident. I would only have to hobble onto a train and people would leap up to offer their seats. I would be struggling through a station and someone would come running up to tell me where the lift was. In bars, complete strangers would offer to carry my drinks back to my table for me. Others would cautiously ask what had happened and if I was alright.

As my limp got better (gradually after about three weeks) people could only tell that I had an injury because I was using crutches. Once, I left my crutches with my friend for a few minutes and someone came over and offered to help *her*. When I no longer needed the crutches I was slightly sad at returning them to the hospital because I knew I would also be losing contact with that helpful and warm side of the English. Sure enough, once the crutches were gone people retreated back into silence and anonymity.

It is often said that the English are "reserved". We don't talk to each other on tube trains, or even make eye contact. The theory is that people are not unfriendly, we just place great importance on the privacy of others, so we don't start talking to them in case they are deep in thought. (Now I come to think of it, it sometimes annoyed me when Americans would start a conversation while I was trying to read a book.)

However, once the English can see a clear reason to talk to you or to offer help, they are very quick to act. Recently I read that the OECD had rated Britain as one of the top five countries in terms of "pro-social behaviour" (helpfulness, basically). One newspaper despatched reporters to test this theory, getting a young woman to pretend to struggle with a heavy suitcase at the bottom of a steep set of steps for example. People of all sorts tried to help, some of them running over despite being headed in the other direction.

If I had read that before my accident, I would probably have cynically assumed that the undercover reporters were helped because they were attractive young women. But from my own experience I know that people were also desperate to help me. That accident helped me realise that behind the often grumpy appearance of the English, they are secretly very nice.

Me and my "lucky" crutches

2

The Little Jar of Englishness

Recently, I was trying to think of something distinctly English, something that applies only to people born and bred in this country. A love of football is common among Englishmen (but then, it is also common among German men). Most English people like drinking tea (but so do the Irish). We are good at forming orderly queues (but so are the Japanese). And so on. Eventually I decided that Englishness was a sort of combination of several things, not all of which were universal or exclusive.

There was one thing, though, that was peculiarly English: a foodstuff called Marmite. I think it's safe to say that every English person has eaten Marmite at some stage in his life and will usually feel quite strongly about it. There is a famous cliché about Marmite that "you either love it or hate it". However, hardly anyone from overseas will have even heard of Marmite. The exception would be people who have done a homestay in England, because most English people have a jar of it in the house.

It's hard to describe Marmite. It's a sticky, almost-black paste that's sold in small jars. It doesn't look very appealing and, some would say, it doesn't taste very nice either. If I had to describe the taste I would probably say "Marmitey", because it's quite distinctive. If pushed, I would add that it tastes a bit salty and gooey. Everybody in England knows it's made from yeast extract, but if you asked them what yeast extract is I suspect they would answer, "It's the stuff Marmite is made from." As far as I know there is only one way to eat Marmite: you spread it thinly on toast.

But Marmite is more than a foodstuff. It's somehow tied up with our sense of national identity. I know it sounds crazy but people seem to think it's their patriotic duty to have a jar of it at home, even if they almost never eat it. This was particularly true for me while I lived overseas. I would make sure to buy Marmite when I visited England from Japan or the US. And then I would open it, eat it once or twice and just leave it in the cupboard. (Sometimes, I would forget I still had a jar I had hardly touched and buy a new one.)

In Australia there is a product called Vegemite which is very similar to Marmite. But you should never say that to an Australian because they are even more protective of Vegemite than the English are of Marmite. Any patriotic Australian will insist their version is better, but it's a bit like arguing "military grey" is a better colour than "ocean grey".

In 2011, there was a story that spread quickly around England. People mailed it to each other and it appeared in the "most viewed" rankings of several online newspapers. The headline read "Denmark bans Marmite".

This caused an equal amount of indignation and confusion. English people couldn't decide whether to exclaim "How dare they?" or "Why on earth would they?" One of the newspaper articles even suggested that banning Marmite was going to make it harder for Denmark to retain skilled foreign workers, as if deprivation of Marmite would force English professionals to flee back to their home country.

It turns out that the Danes prohibit foods that, like Marmite, have been fortified with added vitamins, but the English saw it as a kind

Yeasty, salty Englishness in a jar

of insult to our national pride. I found it odd because probably fewer than one in ten English people eat Marmite regularly. Nevertheless, Marmite looms large in our national consciousness. A British person might say, for example, that "John is a Marmite kind of guy", and people will know it means others will either "love him or hate him".

3

My Unloved Home County

"I am a man from Essex; I am not an Essex Man."

This was a sentence I made up in the early 1990s and used quite a lot. It meant, basically, that although I was born and raised in Essex I didn't consider it to define me as a person.

I forgot about this expression until 2010, when I returned to England. Suddenly I found that when people asked me where I was from I could no longer reply "England" or "London area". To other English people I had to say I was from Essex—and I wasn't too pleased to be put in that position.

Essex, you see, is probably the most unfashionable county in the whole of the United Kingdom. And Romford, where I grew up, is possibly the least fashionable bit of Essex. I am not ashamed to be from Romford. In fact, I like it very much as a place and enjoy visiting it (not only because many of my friends and family still live there). The problem is other people make certain assumptions about you if you are from Essex.

In a sense, Essex is a bit like Saitama: it seems boring compared to the capital city nearby. It doesn't have a reputation for scenic beauty like Kent, another county near London, or a reputation for being wealthy, like Surrey. In America, New Jersey has a similar problem to Essex in that both have a reputation for being cultureless. In Essex, many people think, lower class men speak English badly, swear a lot, drink a lot and get into fights. The women have the reputation of overdressing, drinking heavily and being promiscuous. Both Essex men and women are perceived as being ill-educated and obsessed with money and status symbols.

These stereotypes existed when I was a young man in the early 1990s. There were lots of jokes about "Essex girls", while "Essex Man" was a term used to mean a working-class man who admired Margaret Thatcher (because Essex men reputedly cared more about making money than the well-being of society). People from Essex were "common" and did embarrassing things, according to the clichés. The men were all called "Gaz", drove their cars too fast and wore white socks. The girls were called Sharon (or Tracey), wore too much jewellery and danced around their handbags at nightclubs.

I rather hoped that this reputation would have died down during my years overseas. If anything it seems to have gotten worse, partly thanks to television. There is a popular series, called *The Only Way Is Essex*, about the lifestyles of some stereotypical Essex young people. But I have also had the misfortune recently of watching a "documentary" which secretly filmed people from Romford in the back of a taxi at night. Of course, they were mostly returning from a night out so acted and spoke like people who had been drinking. Another programme was about a young Romford woman with bleached blond hair and a deep suntan whose ambition was "to marry a Premier League footballer". The programme sent her to live with a strict family in Sri Lanka to experience some parental discipline and broaden her horizons. (It was painful to watch.)

I am sure readers can understand why I really hate English people assuming that I am ignorant just because I come from Romford. But I don't just want people to acknowledge that I am intelligent, while continuing with the smug idea that Essex is a bad place full of laughable people.

I don't actually disagree with the fact that there are people in Essex who care little about education, culture or speaking English properly. I have seen that a lot of young men in Essex drink heavily and spend heavily on clothes and cars. But the point is that these are characteristics of the modern-day English as a whole, not just Essex people. It might be nice for people to think that all those embarrassing traits exist only within the borders of Essex, but in fact they are a problem all over England. It hardly matters to any rational observer that these things may be slightly more common in Essex than, say, Buckinghamshire.

So I have decided to change the answer I use when I felt people are pigeonholing me as an "Essex Man". Next time I will say, "I am from Essex. And so are you."

Good question?

4

The Art of Purchasing

It is January 2012 and I have recently undergone possibly the biggest change in my life so far: I have become a homeowner. For well over a year, the search for a house and the purchase process has dominated my life. So I hope readers will understand why I want to impart some of what I experienced.

We sometimes say that moving home is the third most stressful thing that can happen to a person (after divorce and the death of a spouse). By all accounts, I had a relatively straightforward deal. But I still had to learn a new set of skills and concentrate on "acting" correctly throughout.

Firstly, you arrange to view a house you are interested in. Quite often you are shown around by the owner, who is still living at the house. It's quite strange to be in a stranger's house but even weirder that you must ignore the usual rules of politeness and be slightly dismissive about his house ("Oh, this room's a bit dark…") You shouldn't appear too keen and, if possible, should remind the vendor that the economy is in dire straits. All this is necessary because you are effectively beginning the process of negotiating a price. Indeed, it is more important to fake disinterest if you actually really like the house and want to buy it.

You always have to compromise on what you want. Some people prioritise location, some must have a garden and others need "all mod cons". You can't have them all unless you are very rich, so you have to know what you can and can't live without.

Sellers always have an "asking price". But you should never actually pay this price because it is always set unrealistically high. Instead, you must make an "offer" that is much lower. You might think the best thing is to offer what you are prepared to pay, but actually you must offer lower than you are finally prepared to pay. That's because the vendor almost always rejects the first offer. Then you have to decide whether to make a "final offer", and how much to increase it by.

As a buyer, you are torn between the wish not to overpay and the desire not to lose a house you like for the sake of an extra bit of money. I myself had to withdraw from buying a house I loved because the seller would not reduce the price enough. Emotionally that was difficult, but financially it was the right decision.

Even after agreeing a price, you still need to get a surveyor to inspect the property. This is because most houses in England are not newly built and an old house may have problems that are not obvious (subsidence is the most serious, damp is the most common). When this happens, the buyer should ask the seller for *another* reduction. This is quite hard to do because very few people like to keep talking about money, especially if the seller has already reduced the price quite a lot.

The reason it is important to do it all correctly is that house prices in Britain are very high, and negotiating hard can mean a difference of many thousands of pounds. Between 1997 and 2007, house prices rose by a staggering 250% and have barely dropped back from that peak. In the south east of England, I estimate that the average house in South East England costs seven times the average salary. People have to take on a terrifying amount of debt to buy. On the other hand, houses in England generally rise in value in the long term, especially if looked after well. This is very different from Japan, where apartments lose their value over a couple of decades.

The most stressful part for me was that the process from first viewing until exchange of contracts is slow, usually taking between three and six months, and at any stage either side can withdraw for any reason. The seller might get a better offer, lose his job, fall ill or be unable to find a new place to move to. I had some sleepless nights over this.

I actually think that house prices are likely to fall a bit more over the next 18 months. Maybe I should have waited, but in the end it is not only an economic decision but a lifestyle decision. As the great economist J.M. Keynes once said: "In the long run, we are all dead."

The English have a particular obsession with home ownership, and I am no different. Even so, I am surprised at the pride and satisfaction it has given me to become a homeowner. It may not be much of a place (it's not in a prime location, is a bit dark, suffers from damp, requires a lot of modernisation etc.) but I go to sleep knowing that there is a little Victorian house and garden that belongs to me, and I love it.

5

Journeying to Frustration

If I had to say what is the most annoying thing about living in England I would say it is the trains. Our trains are not very reliable, are very expensive and are ridiculously confusing.

For example, if you go to Colchester station and buy a ticket to London (about 90 kilometres away, roughly the same distance as Odawara to Tokyo) it will usually cost you £23.80, as long as it is not during the morning or evening rush hours. But if you book a bit in advance for a specific train on a specific date you will probably be able to buy a ticket for £10, or sometimes even £5. But if you buy the advance ticket and your plans change you cannot change your train or get a refund.

There are lots of different tickets available, some of them logical, some of them absurd. It costs more to travel during the morning rush hour, which has some rationale. But a return ticket is usually only a few pennies more than a single ticket (£23.90). Meanwhile, a "travelcard", which includes all-day use of the London Underground and London buses, usually costs only a bit more (£29.60). The basic "return" ticket is only for journeys made the same day, so if you plan to go in to London and return the next day, you need a different kind of ticket (an "open return", which is more expensive at £34.10).

It's easy to make a mistake with your ticket, but the train companies are unpleasant to anyone who does. If, for example, you buy an advance ticket for the 12:30 express train from Colchester to London but miss it and get the slow train at 12:45 you will be fined if a ticket inspector finds you. The £10 you paid for your initial ticket will be lost; you will be charged £23.80 for the journey; and you will be fined another £23.80 (a total cost of £57.60). There have even been cases when a train is badly delayed and people have boarded the next train that comes along, and still been fined even though they arrive later than scheduled because of the train company's inadequacy. This kind of thing makes it very stressful to use advance tickets, which is why some people avoid them.

People living in England don't like our train system, of course, but at least they have a chance to get used to it. I know to book train tickets in advance whenever I can. And I know that it is relatively cheap (only relatively, I stress) to go in and around London and come back the same day, so I try to cram a lot into one day rather than making several briefer trips. I feel bad for tourists and visitors, who have little chance to work the system effectively.

Recently, I had one of those nightmare journeys that everyone in England has experienced at some point. I wanted to go from Hackney, in east London, to Richmond in the suburbs of west London. Because I had a lot of luggage, I decided to use a route that is slow but requires no change of train. As a precaution, I asked a London transport worker the day before if that train line was meant to be running normally that weekend. He looked at a confusing map, showing dozens of "service alterations" across London, but reassured me my train would be running as usual.

He was wrong. When I got to Hackney station I found that all day those trains would only go halfway, and so I would have to change onto a "replacement bus service" (English people hate to hear those words). When I got to the point where the train stopped, there were no signs telling us which way to the bus stop. When I finally found it, there was no bus waiting for us. Instead we all had to wait about 20 minutes in the wind and cold.

When the bus arrived, I discovered that it

was not actually going to Richmond. Instead, it would trundle through the traffic for a few miles (half of the *rest of the way*) and drop us at an underground station from where we could get a tube train to Richmond. Needless to say, I was pretty annoyed carrying all my bags up and down stairs. And as bad luck would have it I had to wait another 15 minutes for the underground train to arrive to take us the last little bit. A journey that I had expected to take an hour took almost double the time.

I was also worried about my ticket. I had paid for the whole journey but had needed to use my ticket to exit the station when the train stopped halfway. For the rest of my journey, theoretically, I had no valid ticket and you can get fined £50 for travelling without a ticket in London. I didn't actually get fined, but I think some passengers paid a second time to be on the safe side.

The attitude of public transport authorities

in England seems to be that if the passenger can get to his destination they have done their job. So I have come up with an advertising slogan to fit: British trains — an expensive and stressful way to eventually get where you are going.

English trains sometimes arrive on time

6

Pride and Pearl Buttons

Ahead of the 2012 Olympics I spent quite a lot of time exploring east London. Although I grew up in a suburb on that side of London, I didn't visit the "East End" very often. When I went into town, I preferred to head into central or west London. In that, I wasn't unusual. The vast majority of people who come to London do the same. Most of the city's famous attractions are in central London and westwards: the Houses of Parliament, St Paul's Cathedral, Buckingham Palace, the National Gallery, the British Museum, the theatres, the famous shops etc.

But I have come to realise that east London is a fascinating place to visit, and not because of the Olympic Park. East London has a history and culture that make it unique. To pick up one small aspect, it is in east London that the tradition of "pearly kings and queens" started. Until recently, I didn't know much about this tradition but I was fascinated to actually meet and talk to some pearly queens and to learn about them.

East London was traditionally a working-class area of London, and the "pearlies" are a bit like working-class royalty. If you ever see a pearly king you will never forget it. They wear black suits and caps which are decorated elaborately with thousands of gleaming buttons. The suits weigh quite a lot (and, I'm told, are hot in summer and cold in winter). The buttons are made from mother of pearl and are arranged to create patterns and motifs (horseshoes signifying good luck, anchors symbolizing hope etc.) The queens are even more striking visually because they also wear colourful feather hats.

You are most likely to come across a pearly at a celebration, and they are very busy this year (2012) because of street parties and festivities marking the Diamond Jubilee of the "other Queen". They sometimes sing (there are a few sing-along songs that are closely associated with east London). People love to take their photographs, and be in photographs with them. The pearlies do all this to raise money for charity, but they also raise people's spirits.

The tradition was spontaneously devised in the 1870s by a street-sweeper named Henry Croft, himself an orphan. According to folklore, a large consignment of relatively cheap pearl buttons reached London from Japan in the 1860s. London market traders (known as "costermongers") began to wear these buttons to stand out, and as if to say they were the equals of the wealthy ladies who wore real pearls.

Croft began to collect these buttons, which he sometimes found as he cleaned the streets, and sew them into a jacket. One day he put on his completed suit, with hundreds of buttons, and stood on the street asking for donations "all for charity". It moved me to hear that someone so poor himself would make such an effort on behalf of others. And it moved people at that time, too, because costermongers began to join him, devising their own suits and raising money for the poor.

When Croft died in 1930 some 400 pearlies attended his funeral. Today's pearlies are the descendants of those original pearlies because it is a hereditary position. There are even pearly princesses and princes; some of them seventh generation.

East London is changing rapidly. What was once the home of the English working class has also been the first home for waves of immigrants. The area has also been gentrified. There are young architects, artists, graphic designers etc. moving in. The former Truman brewery and the old Spitalfields fruit and vegetable market are now home to galleries and boutique shops, employing artists and fashionistas rather than coopers and porters. For some Londoners, the pearlies are an odd relic of the past. But I found them very uplifting: a symbol of hope and charity, as Mr Croft intended, and of continuity in a changing world.

Some "pearlies" with guests

7

The London Slang Dictionary

A sampling of words that are in common use in London but are not standard English.

Bee's knees (expression)

Meaning "the best", but often used in a slightly mocking negative sense. The origin of the expression is unclear, but it may be a variation of the similar-sounding expression "the business", which has a similar meaning.

Sample sentence: "He spent lots of money on a new suit and now he thinks he's the bee's knees."

Bird (noun)

Girlfriend, or woman. Now falling out of favour because it is considered sexist but still widely used between male friends. Derived from the idea that women are — like birds — attractive, chirpy and (compared to men) small.

Sample sentence: "I usually go out with my mates on Friday night but spend Saturday with my bird."

Boozer (noun)

A pub. Derived from the word "booze", meaning alcoholic drinks.

Sample sentence: "We got kicked out of that boozer once for being too noisy."

Brickie (noun)

A bricklayer. An example of how Londoners create casual nicknames for people in certain jobs. See also "postie" (postman), "sparky" (electrician) and "squaddie" (soldier).

Sample sentence: "Brickies have to work hard but there's good money in it."

Cheers (expression)

In addition to its use as a toast, "cheers" can also mean "thank you" or even "goodbye". Not to be confused with "cheerio", which is used to mean "goodbye" but not "thank you".

Sample sentence: "John told me that you sorted out the tickets for the game. Cheers, I really appreciate it."

Gaff (noun)

Home, or place of residence. Of uncertain origin.

Sample sentence: "Do you want to come round my gaff after the pub? I've recorded *Match of the Day*."

Geezer (noun)

A neutral word for "man", unlike in American English in which it means "old man" and has negative connotations. Sometimes used in the expression "diamond geezer", to mean "reliable friend" or "good guy". See also "bloke", which is used similarly to "geezer", and old-fashioned equivalents "chap" and "fellow".

Sample sentence: "I saw your ex-bird with some geezer last night. Best to forget her."

Go pear shaped (expression)

To go wrong, usually unexpectedly.

Sample sentence: "It was a good evening until someone suggested we have some tequila shots. After that everything went pear shaped."

Have a go (expression)

To criticise or attack, usually verbally but sometimes physically. See also "have a pop", though this more often means a physical attack.

Sample sentence: "I made one little joke about his shirt and now he's telling everyone that I am always having a go at him."

Have the hump (expression)

To be annoyed, usually with another person but sometimes with a situation. Derived from the way people raise their shoulders and lower their chin when irritated, causing their backs to resemble a hump.

Sample sentence: "Why have you got the hump with me? I was only trying to help."

Plonker (noun)

A foolish person. A gentle word to reprimand or mock a friend. Popularised in the 1980s by the television programme *Only Fools and Horses*. See also "wally", which is used in a similar way.
Sample sentence: "I told Dave to take the 86 bus but he got the 68 and ended up in the middle of nowhere. What a plonker."

See a man about a dog (expression)

A euphemism for "go to the toilet". Usually used only by men, mostly in pubs. In the past, people sometimes brought unwanted puppies to a pub to sell or give away, therefore it was not unusual for someone to leave their friends for a moment to "see a man about a dog". The expression was adopted as a euphemism for going to the toilet.
Sample sentence: "You get the beers in. I've got to see a man about a dog."

Sprog (noun)

A child. A casual, affectionate word when used

in reference to your own children, or those of a friend or relative, but not to be used in polite situations or about the children of someone you don't know well. Derived from an old German word.

Sample sentence: "My cousin had three sprogs before he was 25."

Ta (expression)

The most abbreviated way to say "thank you". Used between friends when the favour does not require formal or full thanks. It can be strengthened by saying "ta very much" or "ta muchly", though this is a jokey expression. Not to be confused with "tara" or "ta-ta", used in northern England to mean "goodbye".

Sample sentence: "Pass me the milk, could you? Ta very much."

Take the Mickey (expression)

To make fun of, or kid someone. Someone who is constantly making fun of people is called a

"Mickey-taker". See also the rarer alternative "extract the Michael". Derived from the ruder expression to "take the piss".

Sample sentence: "He's always taking the Mickey. On Saturday he told me Arsenal lost 3-2 when actually they won 1-0."

Wedge (noun)

Money. One of several slang words for money (see also "folding stuff", "dosh", "wad" et al.) Wedge is an old English word for a part of a coin, from the days when a coin could be halved or quartered to represent a smaller sum of money. Often used specifically to refer to a pay packet.

Sample sentence: "Pete's very mean with money. He gets good wedge but never spends any of it."

Zilch (noun)

A casual but emphatic word for "zero". Possibly made by combining the first letter of "zero" with the latter part of "nil" and adding "ch" for vocal emphasis. Sometimes used in the expression "a big fat zilch" for extra impact. Londoners may also say "absolutely nuffink" (a mispronunciation of the word "nothing") for similar purposes.

Sample sentence: "I put a charity collection box in my office last week. When I checked it today we had raised precisely zilch."

8

A Secret, Sometimes Funny Language

When I am with friends from my hometown, especially when we are overseas or in the company of foreigners, we have a sort of secret language that we can use because we grew up in east London. It isn't really a "language" but rather a small part of a dialect, but it can allow people to say something aloud in the presence of others but only be understood by friends.

It is called "cockney rhyming slang", and effectively it was invented as a code to allow the east London working class to talk without being understood by outsiders, including the police (it is believed that it was also used by criminals). It originated in the mid-nineteenth century but has continued to evolve since then.

Today, cockney rhyming slang is used a bit less and understood a bit more widely (you can find it in dictionaries, or look it up online).

A Secret, Sometimes Funny Language

Certainly, there is a core of around 20 or so expressions that are known to most people in Britain, though not to many foreigners even if they speak excellent English.

The "formula" for cockney rhyming slang is both simple and complicated. You take a common set of words that appear together and link them to a word that the last word rhymes with. To take some well-known examples, "dog and bone" means "phone", "jam jar" means "car" and "frog and toad" means "road". It's fairly easy once you know it, but for the uninitiated it is obviously confusing to hear someone say, "He drove a jam jar down the frog and toad."

Another layer of complication comes when the latter part of the expression is dropped (as is often the case). For example if you heard someone say, "Can I have a butcher's?" you would have no chance of just guessing what they meant. (You might have some chance of guessing if they used the full expression "butcher's hook", which is used to mean "look".) Another example of this is "barnet" which means "hair", and comes from "Barnet Fair", a horse fair that was famous in London in the nineteenth century.

Sometimes people may be using rhyming slang without realising it. For example, I used to say "bread" to mean "money", without knowing that it comes from "bread and honey". I think a lot of people say "use your loaf" to mean "think about it", without knowing that "loaf" is short for "loaf of bread" = "head".

Some of my favourite expressions are a product of a particular period but survive beyond it. You might hear someone say that they hurt their "Gregory" playing football. It dates from the time when people would automatically think of the actor Gregory Peck, and therefore means "neck". Today in a pub someone might say, "Get the Britneys in, will you?" It may take a moment, but context should help you guess that "Britney Spears" means "beers".

In modern Britain young men might use this slang to say something they would prefer people didn't hear them say. For example, "too many fridges" would mean "this bar has too many men and not enough women", because "fridge freezer" means "geezer" (a London word for "man"). Or one might say "not sure about the boat race" to mean "that girl seems nice but isn't pretty" ("boat race" = "face").

New rhyming slang can be improvised, and if it is funny and clever can catch on. I enjoy it most when someone spontaneously invents a new phrase. It's fun to do, and fun to "solve" the puzzle. One of my favourites was when a friend said of a tutor with a big beard that he is "quite William and Mary". William and Mary were co-monarchs of England so the names are often used together. My friend used this to mean "hairy".

Another time, a friend looked at his baby

son and said, "Oh no! He's done another Douglas". There was a famous politician called Douglas Hurd in the Thatcher years, so my friend used his name to mean "turd". I worked it out in seconds. So just as we realised that he was going to have to change a smelly nappy, we were both reduced to happy laughter.

"Jam jars" on the "frog and toad"

9

The National Obsession

Around 150 years ago, one of the most important meetings ever took place in a London pub. I use the word "important" with some reservations — this wasn't exactly a pivotal moment in history — but there is no doubt that the meeting has had a large impact on the lives of millions of people since.

It was in 1863 at the Freemasons' Tavern that the Football Association first convened and began to codify the laws of the game of football. It's highly appropriate that the meeting should have happened in a pub, because football has been discussed, analysed and watched in pubs ever since. There is almost a symbiotic relationship between pubs and football. Beer and "the game" are two preoccupations of the average British man. I am not unusual in that some of my happiest moments have been when

I have a pint in hand and a game to watch.

Versions of football had existed before 1863, both in England and other countries. But it was at this London meeting that the present-day sport began to take shape. One of the most important decisions was that "hacking" would no longer be permitted. In other words, it would now be a foul to kick or otherwise impede a player who had the ball. Another was that players would not be permitted to run with the ball in their hands. This was the origins of the split between football and rugby. The rules of football have been tweaked and elaborated greatly over the many decades since, but the game played across the world today clearly derives from those rules laid down in London in the middle of the nineteenth century.

Football is our "national pastime". I remember a sports journalist once joking that the English cared about two sports: "football… and the others". Not everyone in England follows football, but if you don't have any interest you will find yourself excluded from a lot of conversations. If you state that you don't like football, you are taking a position that will alienate you from a lot of people (though some people will admire you). I sometimes wish I didn't like football but I find I cannot help it. It can be an expensive hobby, it can be heart-breaking when your team lose, it is often annoying because the players are extravagantly paid and don't seem loyal… but I still find myself gripped by the unscripted "theatre" that football provides.

At times, it seems like football is the religion of the English masses. Certainly more Englishmen watch football games than go to church at the weekend. And the language some fans use about football has a religiosity. A brilliant player is called a "god", a beautiful goal is called "divine" and fans will intone that "the team is bigger than any one individual". It is not uncommon that fans ask that, when they die, their ashes be scattered across the pitch of their favourite team. The clubs of course have to refuse these requests, but ahead of games will announce the "sad passing of a lifelong fan…"

Personally, I try not to take football too seriously. I think that people who watch every game and rank football as more important than their families or jobs (as some do) are misguided. But I also can't deny that a great win can make me happy when other things are going badly, or that losing a game to a bitter rival will sour an otherwise nice day. As a friend of mine once put it, "It's funny how a decision you make when you are seven years old, to support one team rather than another, will affect your moods for the rest of your life."

That decision will also affect your identity in unexpected ways. I happened to choose Arsenal because when I was a boy they had a lot of Irish players so I thought they were the team who represented me as "London Irish". But today, Arsenal have no Irish players and instead have a reputation of being a rather "French" club (with a French manager and a lot of French and Francophone players). In earlier times, Arsenal were the club of the wealthier and Conservative-voting working-class Londoners (because they were originally formed from workers at a munitions factory).

We sometimes talk about football fans as belonging to particular tribes. It has certainly deepened some of my friendships to discover a shared support of Arsenal. In England, people often greet each other by saying "Did you see the game last night?" or "What do you think of that new player?" When their team wins, men sometimes hug each other (which they almost never do in everyday life).

It can also be problematic. I have friends who support Spurs, the traditional rivals of my team. Recently, I had a builder working at my house and he mentioned he was a Liverpool fan. I decided to hide my framed photograph of the Arsenal manager, in case it made the builder dislike me and do a poor job.

Certainly, Englishmen sometimes emote about football to a surprising degree, talking about how much they "love" their team, whereas they might never publicly admit to loving their wives. Or they will say they "hate" another team.

A famous football manager once joked that "football isn't a matter of life and death... it's more important than that". It isn't, of course, but it is a major fact of life in this country.

Arsenal Stadium: holy ground?

10

How to Buy a Pint of Beer

When I came back to England, I realised that something that is second nature to me is full of cultural quirks. I noticed that buying a beer in this country has its own rules and rituals, and that these are not obvious to people from elsewhere. Even worse, because the rules are so normal to us, we often don't realise they need to be explained. And we get annoyed if anyone fails to follow the correct procedure. So I thought I would try to explain some of the basics of this apparently simple business.

The first step is to enter the pub, obviously. This is slightly more intimidating than you might expect because very often you can't see inside the pub from the street. (The windows were traditionally frosted to let people drink without being spotted from the street by wives or bosses.) But take a deep breath and step inside, because the pub is one of the great British experiences.

Once inside, do not stand at the door waiting for someone to greet you or escort you to a table. There are no waiters. Find a table you like and claim it. But don't sit there waiting for someone to take your order, even if there is a menu on the table. To get a beer you need to go up to the bar and order it. In London I have quite often seen tourists sitting at their table for several minutes waiting for service before they work out how everyone else is getting their drinks.

At the bar there is no *apparent* queuing system. People will spread along the length of the bar and hope to get served. But it only *seems* like a free-for-all. In fact, we have a clumsy but functioning system of waiting. The customers almost unconsciously note who has been waiting longer than them and who arrived after them. It is very bad manners to get served out of turn. The bar staff will try to serve people in the right order, but at busy times it is hard to be sure. So they rely on self-policing by the customers. "Who's next?" they ask. You should only raise your hand if it is you. If in doubt, check with other customers by asking, "Were you before me, mate?"

You mustn't treat staff at a pub like waiters. So you don't snap your fingers to get attention or ask, "Can I get some service please?" It is better to attract attention by smiling and making eye contact or, if necessary, holding out a folded ten pound note to indicate that you wish to buy a beer. In return, the staff will usually not call you "sir", but talk in a more friendly, informal manner.

You also do not directly tip bar staff. Most people don't actually tip bar staff at all, but if you wish to do so you shouldn't give cash. Instead, offer to buy them a drink ("Have one yourself") when you are buying your drink.

They will almost certainly say, "Thank you, I will have it later" and keep a pound or two from your change. So it is in fact a cash tip but disguised as a friendly offer of a drink.

You can't just ask for "A beer please" as you can in Japan and some other countries. There will be many different beers and you have to choose one. In quiet pubs, you can ask for a recommendation. But don't try this in busy town-centre pubs. They will want you to decide quickly what you want. You could just look at the taps along the bar and pick one at random, but you should remember there are various *types* of beer in England: lager, bitter, stout, cider etc. If you know what type you want to try, you can say, "a lager please" and they will either serve you one or tell you what lagers they have for you to choose from.

If you just don't specifically say otherwise, you will automatically be served a pint—the traditional 568 ml English glass. This may seem a lot to some people, but is the standard size to the English (we will usually drink several of these). You can ask for a half pint, but English people rarely do this because they prefer not to have to keep going back to the bar for more.

There are a few phrases that you might hear in a pub that are confusing. "What's your poison?" is a jokey expression meaning "What would you like to drink?" The bar staff might ask you this, or someone who is offering to buy you a drink. (Alcohol is a sort of poison, and drinkers are making light of this by asking each other what form of poison they want.)

You might also be asked, "Is that dead?" by a bartender. Again, don't be alarmed. He means "Have you finished with that drink?" Some people like to drain every drop from their glass, but others might leave a little bit. So staff use this unusual expression to check before they collect the glasses.

Another key word in pubs is "round". This

is the system whereby people buy beer for each other in turn. So one person buys for his friends, then the next drinks are bought by someone else in the group and so on. If someone buys you a drink, it is polite to offer them back with the words "I believe it's my round". If you reach this stage, you have mastered elementary pub manners.

Don't just ask for "a beer"

11

A Song for England

One of the unusual things about the United Kingdom is that although it is one nation it consists of more than one country. England, Scotland, Wales and Northern Ireland each have their own identities and they have their own sports teams, so we sometimes have "international" games featuring sportsmen only from the UK. Scotland plays England at rugby, for example, or Northern Ireland might play Wales at football.

When nations compete at sport, the national anthem of each team is normally played before the game. So the situation for UK teams is a bit strange. "God Save the Queen" is the official anthem of the whole UK, but Scotland and Wales also have alternative anthems that can be used instead: respectively, "Flower of Scotland" and "Land of My Fathers". At the moment, England and Northern Ireland both use "God Save the Queen". People sometimes wonder if the same anthem is played twice when the two teams meet. (Actually, it is only played once.)

"Flower of Scotland" is a memorable, easy-to-sing piece that commemorates a Scottish victory over the English in battle in 1314. People sometimes think it is an ancient song but actually it dates back only to 1967, written by a folk band called The Corries. "Land of My Fathers" is a stirring piece, which is always sung in the Welsh language (and is therefore correctly called "Hen Wlad Fy Nhadau").

Anyway, my point is that as an Englishman I am jealous. Scotland and Wales have their own powerful, bespoke anthems but we are stuck with "God Save the Queen", which I simply don't like very much. It's not a very interesting tune, it doesn't "belong" to the English exclusively and its lyrics don't inspire me. I don't dislike the

Queen, I just don't think a song praising her is the most appropriate way to express the identity of England. I know I am not alone in this point of view because sometimes the English discuss choosing an alternative anthem.

Many people argue the case for "Land of Hope and Glory". Certainly, it is a powerful and famous song that was composed by an Englishman, Edward Elgar, with lyrics by A. C. Benson. The problem is that the lyrics reflect the naked imperialism of the period in which they were written (1902). Basically, they call for the UK to extend its empire: "Wider still and wider shall thy bounds be set; God, who made thee mighty, make thee mightier yet." So the song is rather "jingoistic" and doesn't seem well-suited to the present day.

A similar drawback affects another well-loved song, "I Vow to Thee My Country". The beautiful tune is adapted from Gustav Holst's "Jupiter" (from *The Planets*) and the lyrics were adapted from a poem by Cecil Spring-Rice, a British diplomat. The first verse is the problem, since it is blindly nationalistic. It calls for men to love their country unconditionally and to be willing to die for it. I think the song is redeemed somewhat by its last verse, which reminds us that there is "another country"—the kingdom of heaven—which we should also serve.

Probably, the most popular candidate for an English anthem is "Jerusalem", which sets the words of a poem by William Blake to strident music. The interesting thing to me is that the poem has a certain ambiguity, so people of various philosophies like it. It poses the question (not answered) of whether Jesus ever visited England. Then it declares a resolve to make England a better country. Right-wing people like it, because it implies England is a special country, beloved by God. Left-wing people see it as a call to create a "new Jerusalem" (a more just society).

There are also a few slightly eccentric suggestions. Rugby fans like "Swing Low, Sweet Chariot" (which they sing during games). However I don't think it is a good idea because it is a Negro spiritual, a Christian song written by an African American in the nineteenth century and therefore not English in origin. Furthermore, it is *only* popular with rugby fans. A few football fans might jokingly counter that they prefer one of the songs they have adopted: the theme tune from *The Great Escape*, a film about the escape of Allied POWs from a prison in Germany during World War II. The song is very catchy and upbeat, but it was written by an American for a film made by Americans.

However, the football fans might be on to something. I do sometimes think the English could avoid a lot of trouble if they chose a song with no words. Anthems don't *have* to have lyrics (the Spanish national anthem doesn't). One option for England would be "Nimrod", from Elgar's *Enigma Variations*. It's a mysterious, uplifting piece that is often played at memorial services and the like. Since it has no lyrics, people can impose whatever meaning they like on it. I imagine that it expresses the quiet resolve of the English people. But another person might imagine it portrays the subtle beauty of our landscape. In other words, it might be a nicely enigmatic anthem for a people who don't always agree on who they are.

12

London's "Other" Waterway

If you asked people what is the most important waterway in London I am sure that almost all of them would say the River Thames. But there is another fascinating waterway — the Regent's Canal — that deserves to be better known and is in fact enjoying something of a renaissance.

The canal dates back to the early nineteenth century, when it was built to facilitate the movement of goods across London. It stretches for almost 14 kilometres, from near Paddington in west London to Limehouse in east London, where it meets the Thames. Naturally, when the freight industry shifted towards road and rail the canal fell into relative disuse. By the 1960s, it seemed to be a relic of an earlier age.

Despite this decline, the Regent's Canal is one of the best things about London, in my opinion. I am a recent convert, having only discovered the canal in 2010 but since then I have walked along it many times — once covering its whole span in a long afternoon.

The first thing I would say about the Regent's Canal is that it's very different from the Thames. The Thames is a wide, tidal river with dramatic views and grand bridges. The canal is narrow and quiet with comparatively little scenery. These things are part of the attraction. Along stretches of the canal, you could almost forget you are in London, there being few buildings visible and little noise from traffic.

Another important thing about the Regent's Canal is that, like canals all over Britain, it has a towpath running alongside it because barges in the old days were pulled (or "towed") by horses that walked along the bank. This is different from many other cities such as Venice or Edo-period Tokyo where boats were traditionally punted or rowed. Towpaths were effectively made redundant by the invention of engines, but the happy outcome is that today those towpaths are ideal for walkers and cyclists.

For a long time, the only people who used towpaths were ramblers and perhaps a few local people walking their dogs. Today, though, commuters are increasingly likely to make use of the Regent's Canal towpath as they walk or cycle to work. It makes a pleasant contrast to London's overcrowded and expensive public transport.

Certain sections of the Regent's Canal are known and enjoyed by a lot of people. For example, the canal goes through Camden where there is a famous market including many food stalls. People like to eat their food sitting by the canal. Or there is the area called Little Venice, where the Regent's Canal meets the Grand Union Canal (which continues all the way to Birmingham, over 200 kilometres to the north). The canal also branches off at Little Venice to the Paddington Basin, a spot where boats used to dock and unload. So at this location there is a convergence of waterways which makes it a nice place to stroll or stop and read a book.

However, as much as I like Camden and Little Venice, I don't think that just visiting these spots is the best way to experience the Regent's Canal. Rather, I suggest travelling along it. As you walk along the changing scenery reveals itself to you. At the Paddington Basin the view is of offices, shops and restaurants. At other points, the canal banks are green, leafy and shaded. There are usually crowds of people when you pass through Camden, but within a few minutes you will be almost alone again. I particularly like how the canal cuts through London Zoo: on one side there are exotic birds, on the other hyenas. As you move into east London, the "canalside" becomes more industrial.

I would of course love to travel the canal

by boat; after all, that is what it was designed for. The old narrow boats that used to ply the canals of Britain are among the most beautiful vehicles ever created. They are traditionally painted and ornately decorated, so that each one is distinctive. What particularly attracts me is that they are not designed to go fast. These days they are fitted with diesel engines, not horse-drawn, but even so they don't go much faster than walking pace. Furthermore, it can take quite a while to pass through a lock. So, on a narrow boat you have to adapt to a gentler pace of life.

It seems that a lot of people share my love of narrow boats. People hire them for holidays, or even buy them and use them to travel the country. In recent years they have even become a popular form of housing. Property prices in London are absurdly expensive, so some people prefer to buy a narrow boat to live on, mooring it somewhere in London. I have a friend who did this, and he says that one great attraction is that he can relocate his home if he changes job or even if he just wants a change of scene.

It must have seemed at one stage that the canal served no real purpose, after it ceased to be a viable way to transport goods. But today it is a valuable man-made resource used for commuting, for living and for recreation. It is part of London, not just part of its history.

Aboard a canal boat

13

Talking About Weather

The English talk about the weather a lot. We often greet friends by commenting on the weather or use the weather as a way to start a conversation with a stranger. On the surface, it may appear that we are complaining about the weather. For example, if it is pouring rain we might turn to the person next to us at the bus stop and say, "Typical, eh?" with a shake of the head. Or if the wind suddenly picks up while we are having a picnic, blowing everything around, we might say to our friends, "It would have to be windy *today*, wouldn't it?"

But, actually, I don't think people are really complaining. They are mostly consoling each other, resignedly accepting the situation and emphasising that at least we are all sharing the inconvenience of bad weather. It would be very unusual for someone to say something genuinely negative, such as "I am utterly sick of all this rain and cold."

A lot of the time we even joke about the weather. When it is cold, we might ask a friend, "Is it cold enough for you?" Obviously no one would want it to be colder, so this is a bit of gentle irony. Or if there was a little bit of sun on a cloudy day we might say, "I thought there was a danger of getting a bit of sunshine there." Again, it is just slightly playful to suggest that we feel threatened by the possibility of some sunshine.

Each year at the end of March we move our clocks forward by one hour; the start of what we call British Summer Time (as opposed to Greenwich Mean Time from October to March). Since it is usually still quite cold and rainy in March, this prompts quite a lot of joking in Britain. For a week or so, people will be heard commenting, "So this is Summer Time, is it?"

What interests me is that the English

talk about the weather a lot even though our weather is generally very mild. London is not a really cold city like Moscow. We don't have hurricanes, a rainy season or high humidity. The English summer is, in my view, one of the nicest in the world with long, bright evenings and not too much heat.

Strangely, the one time when the English do complain a bit about the weather is when they decide it is too hot. They will call it a "heat wave" if it is over 30 degrees centigrade for more than a few consecutive days. People will say they feel like they are "withering" in the heat. It always seemed comical to me to hear that because I know how much more hot and humid it gets in Tokyo and New York.

We experienced just such a "heat wave" this summer (2013) and for the first time I had some understanding of why the English dislike the heat so much. It's because England isn't really designed to deal with hot weather.

Most of our underground trains and stations, for example, don't have air conditioning and it gets brutally hot down there. The English aren't used to air conditioning anyway, so even when they can use it — in cars, for example — they ruin the effects by opening the windows. They think the breeze will cool the car.

Nor is this sort of ignorance a "new" problem. The Victorians had a primitive form of air conditioning called sash windows. These windows, which are common in English houses from the period, open from two ends. In hot weather, you should pull the top window down part way and put the bottom window up part way. This took advantage of the natural circulation of air, allowing hot air out at the top and cooler air in at the bottom. Unfortunately, many people don't grasp the idea so only open the bottom window. Even worse, sometimes people paint the windows with thick paint so that they no longer open at both ends.

English people also don't know to maintain themselves in hot weather. When we are thirsty, or when we return home tired, it is usual to drink a hot cup of tea. Many people do this even in the middle of summer, apparently unaware that this may be counter-productive. It is only recently in England that it became acceptable for men to wear short trousers and sandals when it is hot. A generation ago it would have been considered unmanly, and I admit that I am of the old school and would never wear shorts in the town however hot it is.

Recently, I heard a sad but funny story. A new type of bus was launched in London which had air conditioning for comfort, and sealed windows to stop people from unhelpfully opening them when it was hot. The problem was that the system broke down when the outside temperature rose above normal levels, causing the inside of the bus to heat up to 30 degrees plus. They were soon dubbed "moving saunas", a phrase which I think captures the English talent for combining a complaint with a joke.

14

The Accidental Gardener

Two years ago I bought a house. It wasn't actually the house I wanted to buy — the one I most liked was a bit too expensive — but family and friends consoled me by pointing out that the house I got was far better because it had a small garden. They cheerfully told me that I could sit outside on nice days, have barbecues, grow vegetables and so on.

I wasn't so sure. I have never had a garden of my own before and on the few occasions I have had even house plants I have managed to kill them either by not watering them or by watering them too much. I was worried that having a whole garden would be a major headache that was doomed to end in failure.

Certainly, I have since had my share of failures. I attempted to grow rhubarb because it is a famously strong plant that requires little attention. I love rhubarb pie and dreamed of making it from my own garden. I watered the rhubarb lightly every few days and all seemed to be going well until it was trampled when a new shed was being installed in my garden. I bought some herbs but these were killed by a freezing cold snowy spell (in April!) I decorated the garden with solar lights but these kept getting blown over by the wind and knocked over by various visitors (human and animal). I desperately wanted to adopt a hedgehog — by creating a space that would be ideal for one to move into — but I couldn't bear it if somehow my bad luck caused the poor animal to die.

On the other hand, I have had some successes (though I cannot really claim credit for them). This year (2013), for example, I found that the apple tree at the end of my garden has produced dozens of hefty apples. Typically when there is an apple tree in someone's garden it produces only "cooking apples" (i.e. apples that are too sour to eat without adding sugar and which are therefore only suitable for pies or jam). My apples are a bit tart but perfectly edible. Incredibly, I only realised this year that another tree at the foot of the garden is a plum tree which this summer yielded a small crop of delicious sweet plums. Here and there, blackberries grow through the bushes, so in August and September I ate breakfasts featuring combinations of these three fruits.

To get an English garden into really good shape, it requires regular attention. Since I am often away I haven't been able to nurture it properly. Even when I am at home I sometimes let weeks pass without doing any gardening. This allows certain plants to take over. The grass grows to knee height and the buddleia and honeysuckle begin to intrude into the spaces of other plants. I am, at least, slowly learning about the nature of domestic gardens because a year ago I wouldn't have known the name "buddleia", or that it is sometimes called "butterfly bush" because it attracts so many butterflies. The honeysuckle attracts bees and the long grass attracts cats, I have also learned.

There are times when I have considered the garden a burden. Cutting back all the excess growth in summer can be a chore. This summer was unusually hot and dry and I felt obliged to go out at night to give the plants a bit of water. Frequently, I would tread on a slug or a snail (the gardener's enemy) which is a very unpleasant thing to happen. But little by little it seems I have formed an attachment to my garden. For example, one day I found myself reading a newspaper article on apple trees (I learned that I had been picking mine too early, as a cold and rainy June meant I should have waited a few weeks longer). I also bought a book on gardening and find myself dipping in to it from time to time. I considered growing burdock (because I wanted to make gobo salad like I used to eat in Japan) but discovered that in England it is considered a very troublesome weed.

As I write this, it is early evening and very often at this time a blackbird will sit in a tree nearby and sing its little heart out. I had never listened to a blackbird sing before I moved here but it is the most beautiful, peaceful thing I can imagine. When I hear it, I find myself thinking that it was a lucky thing I managed to get this house with its small, untidy, badly managed garden.

In need of some attention...

15

A Peculiarly British Alien

Recently I was watching a live BBC television programme on which it would be revealed who would be the next person to hold a certain important position. It wasn't a broadcast about the new leader of a political party, or any government office or even about the new manager of a football team. It was a programme unveiling which actor would next play a television character called Dr Who.

It struck me as strange because Dr Who is hardly known outside the UK, but in this country he is significant enough that there was an entire programme dedicated to the "news" that a different actor would be portraying him soon. In the weeks before this, I remember that several of the newspapers were speculating about who should be the new Dr Who and even some commentators explaining why it should be one actor or another.

I think I should explain about Dr Who. He is the hero of a BBC drama (of the same name) which was invented long before I was born; it first aired in 1963 and there have since been some 800 episodes. The Doctor, as he is often called, is a time traveller who speeds through space and across eras saving planets from destruction and fighting evil alien races. Although he is theoretically from the planet Gallifrey, he speaks with a British accent and has a recognizably British character (in his sense of humour, for example, or his eccentricities). In short, he is a sort of science fiction version of James Bond.

As a child growing up in the 1970s, I would watch *Doctor Who* every week with a mixture of wonder and terror. It could be genuinely scary, particularly when the enemy he was facing was the Daleks. The Daleks are a ruthlessly evil race of creatures who live inside metallic armour shells and scream "Exterminate! Exterminate!" in robotic voices before killing anyone who opposes them. I and millions of other boys watched *Doctor Who* "peeking from behind the sofa", as the expression has it.

Of course, the idea behind *Doctor Who* is commonplace: There is a danger that most people know little of and are powerless to resist. Along comes a brave and brilliant individual to fight it. He faces overwhelming odds and the situation seems hopeless. But finally, cathartically, he wins through and we viewers feel a little bit lifted and cheered.

But Dr Who is a particularly British icon. His main characteristic is that he will always protect the weak from bullying, aggressive types. He doesn't particularly care for recognition (often, the people of the planet he saves will not even know they were in danger) and he has a kind of stubborn resolve. In this sense, Dr Who is the personification of the British people as we like to see ourselves.

He is also a something of a unifying figure. In Britain, he is almost universally liked (unlike, say, our political leaders). People of all ages and all regions like the programme, even if not all of us watch it regularly. I recently had a long discussion with a seven-year-old boy about Dr Who and — unusually — we were both equally interested in the conversation. We discussed who was our favourite Dr Who, the scariest enemy, the best assistant (Dr Who always has an assistant, usually a British woman) etc.

The Doctor never dies, though he does "regenerate" from time to time. Each regeneration requires a new actor, and Dr Who has now been played by 11 different actors (and the era of the twelfth Doctor is now here). Each actor brings a slightly different nuance to the character and most British people have a favourite Doctor. It is probably more common in Britain to hear men debate their favourite Dr Who actor than their favourite James Bond actor.

For a long time there was no *Doctor Who*. It suffered from falling viewing figures in the 1980s and there were no new television episodes broadcast between 1989 and 2005. Its revival was greeted with great excitement and for most people it was a mystery why it took so long to return. *Doctor Who* is a brilliant creation. The theme music is electrifying. Some of the monsters, such as the Daleks and the Cybermen, are as memorable as Godzilla or King Kong. And Dr Who has the best mode of transport ever invented: the TARDIS. Not only can this magic ship fly through time and space, it is huge on the inside but on the outside it is only as big as a telephone box. In fact, the TARDIS is disguised as a police telephone box, which was a handy form of camouflage when the first series began.

I no longer watch *Doctor Who* weekly, though I watch it occasionally for nostalgic reasons. But I must confess that it was no accident that

I was watching when the new Doctor was unveiled. Dr Who is not just part of my childhood but a living national institution. As a Briton, I wanted to know the job of portraying him was in safe hands.

Profile

Colin Joyce was born in 1970 in Essex, one of England's less cultural regions. He studied Ancient and Modern History at Oxford University before deciding that he wanted to learn a second language. Unfortunately, he happened to choose Japanese and was appalled to find that the grammar was all different from English and the words were hard to remember.

He lived in Kobe as a student then Urawa and Tokyo for a total of almost fifteen years. He stayed so long partly because he didn't want to leave until he could do more than ask for directions in Japanese, partly because he enjoyed life in Japan and partly because every time he made a plan to leave he would be offered an interesting job.

After a stint as a (not very good) English teacher at a prefectural high school, he worked as an editor and reporter for *Newsweek Japan* magazine and as the Tokyo correspondent for the *Daily Telegraph*, Britain's leading quality newspaper.

He went to New York in 2007 for three years, where he developed a love of Brooklyn, a taste for American craft beers and a profound distaste for certain American expressions.

He is the author of several books based on his experiences in three countries. Three of these are available in English: *How to Japan*, *An Englishman in N.Y.* and *Let's England*.

He currently lives in Colchester which is the only place other than London to have ever been capital of Britain. Unfortunately, that brief peak in Colchester's fortunes was around 2,000 years ago under the Romans.

He is a freelance journalist and author; and one of Essex's most talented writers, though he admits that the competition isn't very fierce.

はじめに

　海外に長く住むというのは奇妙な体験だ。ぼくはまだ20代初めのころにイギリスを離れ、戻ってきたのは2010年だったから、それまでの20年間のほとんどを日本とアメリカで過ごしたことになる。

　その間にもイギリスには何度も帰ったが、それだけ長く離れていると、自分の国にいるときでも自分がどこかよそ者のように思えた。少なくとも、ほとんどのイギリス人とはちょっと違う人間になった。

　まったくおかしな話だが、イギリスから離れている時間が長くなるほど、ぼくの「イギリス人らしさ」は重要なものになっていった。人に紹介されるときは「こちらはコリン、イギリス人」と言われる。イギリスの何かについて、あるいは何かをするときのイギリス式のやり方について聞かれることはとても多かった。友だちからの気軽な質問だったらまだいいが、ときにぼくは「イギリス人ジャーナリスト」として発言を求められ、ぼくの言葉が活字になることもあった。

　ときどき、自分はまだ本当にイギリス人なのだろうかと思ったりもした。たとえばぼくは、自分が東京の街を熟知していることに気づいた。自分の足で、自転車や電車で、

東京のあらゆるところを探索した。けれどもロンドンでは、一度も足を踏み入れたことのない地域がいくつもあった。ぼくは日本のあちこちをずいぶん旅行したが、イギリスではイングランドの南東部から出ようという気にはそれほどならなかった。

　自分の中に文化の面で変化があったのではないかとも思った。ぼくは自分が「何者でないか」は知っていた。ぼくは日本人ではなかったし（日本で10年以上も楽しく暮らしても）、アメリカ人でもなかった（あの国に３年住んでも）。ぼくは海外に住んだ経験が自分の視野を広げ、人生をより面白くしてくれたと思う。でも同時に、少しイギリス人らしくなくなったことで、よりどころのようなものを失ったとも感じていた。では、ぼくはいったい「何者だった」のだろう？

　イギリスに対するぼくの見方は、「とても愛国的」と「とても批判的」の間を揺れ動いた。新聞で読んだことや友人に聞いた話が、よくも悪くもぼくに大きな影響を与えた。それはおそらく、イギリスに住んでいれば経験するもっと幅広いものごとから切り離されたところで、そういう話を耳にしていたからだと思う。政治スキャンダルのニュースにうんざりしていたのは、その一方で淡々とまじめに仕事をしているイギリスの政治家もたくさんいるということを、ぼくが忘れていたからだ。あるいは、すばらし

いコメディー番組がテレビで始まったことを知って、それがイギリスの文化的な豊かさを示す証拠のように思ったのは、実際にイギリスでテレビのチャンネルをチャカチャカ変えて、「リアリティー」番組や料理番組、バカな「タレント」の番組などなど、いかにひどいものしか流れていないかを目にしていなかったからだ。

　国を離れた者は、離れた日の時点で凍結された国のイメージを持ちつづけるといわれることがある。ぼくの場合は必ずしもそうではなく、イギリスの変化が激しすぎて、ついていけないようにも思えた。1年ぶりに帰っただけでも、イギリスではものごとが微妙に、けれどもこちらの落ち着きがなくなるほど変化していることがあった。

　ようやくぼくは、解決策はイギリスに帰ること、そして半分はわけがわからず、半分はよく知っているこの国と向き合うことしかないとわかった。若いときに海外に出たのは、外国語を学び、ほかの国を経験したかったからだ。次は、自分の国について学ぶという「新しい」経験をしたいと思った。

　この本に収めた文章は、もともとNHK『ラジオ英会話』のテキストに掲載されたものだ。書いた期間は3年にわたっており、イギリスに帰っていささか混乱している時期から始まっている。いま読み返すと、ちょっとした旅をした気にもなる。ぼくは自分の国に住んでいることに少しず

つ慣れていき、これらの文章を月に1度書いていた。ときには、読者のみなさんがいちばん関心を持ってくれそうなことを書こうとした。ときには、自分にとって最も関心があることを書かせてもらった。あとはそのときどきに、いちばん気になったこと（たとえば、イギリスの電車のひどさだとか）を書いた。そのほうが、イギリスに住むというのはどんな感じなのかを生々しくお伝えできると思ったからだ。

この本は多くの人に支えられて生まれた。とくに編集担当の奥村奈美子は、ここに収めた文章をぼくが書いていたときに、忍耐と激励を惜しまずにつき合ってくれた。イギリスには詳しいのに、ぼくの目から見たことを自由に書かせてくれる編集者と仕事ができたのは幸せだった。中野毅も支えになってくれた。翻訳担当の森田浩之は、いつもながら気配りに満ちた仕事をしてくれ、作業途中の原稿をぼくに脇からのぞかせてくれもした（ほとんどの翻訳者は著者との間でそんなことをしない）。

ぼくがロンドンに住んでいるわけでもないのに、エッセイとこの本のタイトルがなぜ *London Calling* なのか、と思う人もいるだろう。かつてBBCは、海外向けのラジオ放送をこの言葉で始めていた。ぼくがBBCのようにイギリスを代表する声だと言いたいわけではなく、自分がイギリスから海外に向けて、ある意味、メッセージを発信して

いるという構図が気に入ったのだ。それにぼくがわりと気に入っているポップソングに、ザ・クラッシュの「ロンドン・コーリング」がある。この本の前に出版したエッセイ集 *An Englishman in N.Y.* もポップソングのタイトル（こちらはスティングだ）を借用していたから、そのつながりも気に入っている。

　最後になるが、*London Calling* というタイトルには個人的な思い入れもある。海外に暮らしていたときは、いくらその国での生活を楽しんでいても、イギリスに帰りたいという思いにつねに悩まされた。ぼくはいつも、自分の国がぼくを「呼んでいる（calling）」ことを感じていた。

1

イギリス人は親切だ

　イギリスに帰ってまもなく、ぼくはたいしたことはないけれど面倒なけがをした。サッカーをやっていて脚の筋肉をひどく伸ばしてしまい、チームメイトに抱えられてフィールドを出るというありさまだった。タイミングは最悪だった。翌日にはニューヨークから友だちが来ることになっていて、1週間ほどあちこち観光に行く予定を立てていたからだ。それなのに、ぼくは数百メートルも歩けなくなってしまったのだ。

　ぼくはこのけがが、ひと晩で奇跡的に回復することを願ったが、眠ったあとには痛みと腫れが増していた。たいしたけがではなく、自然に治ることはわかったけれど、ぼくは自分がとても不運だと感じたものだ。

　しかし数カ月が過ぎた今、ぼくはあのけがが「幸運」なものだったと思っている。もちろん友人が遊びに来ている間は非常に不便だったが、同時にぼくが生まれたイギリスの人々のことを再認識するすばらしいきっかけになった。というのも、みんな突然、ぼくにとてもやさしくしてくれたからだ。信じられないくらいやさしかった、と言ってもいい。

　ぼくはイギリス人が特別に親切だなどと思ったことはな

かった。これまでの人生で不愉快な人にたくさん出会っている。ひとつには、ぼくが特別に親切で礼儀正しいわけではないことで知られる町で育ったためだ。日本に住んでいたときには、日本人はイギリス人に比べて、なんて礼儀正しい人たちだろうと思わずにいられなかった。アメリカに住んでいたときには、アメリカ人はイギリス人にはありえないくらいあけっぴろげで愛想がいいと思ったものだ。イギリスを離れている時間が長くなるにつれて、ぼくはイギリス人のことをよく思わなくなっていき、もう一度イギリス人の中で暮らすこれからの日々が正直言って楽しみなことばかりではなくなっていた。

けれども、そんな思いがこのけがで変わった。ぼくが足を引きずりながら電車に乗ると、まわりの人たちがすぐに立ち上がって、ここに座りなさいと言ってくれる。駅でまごついていると誰かがすぐに駆け寄ってきて、エレベーターはあっちだと教えてくれる。バーに行けば、見も知らぬ人がぼくのテーブルまで飲み物を運ぼうと言ってくれる。ほかにもたくさんの人が「どうしたの？ 大丈夫？」と、心配そうに尋ねてくれた。

けががよくなってくると（3週間ほどたつと、だんだん回復してきた）、ぼくがけがをしていることがまわりにわかる理由は、松葉杖を使っていることだけになってきた。あるとき、ぼくは松葉杖を友だちにほんの何分か預けたこ

とがあった。そうしたら知らない人が駆け寄ってきて、何かできることはないかと彼女のほうに言ってきた。松葉杖がいらなくなって病院に返すときには、少しだけ寂しく思ったものだ。これを返してしまったら、イギリス人の親切で温かい部分に触れることもなくなってしまうとわかっていたからだ。案の定、松葉杖がなくなると、まわりの人々は沈黙と匿名の世界に戻っていってしまった。

　イギリス人は「控えめ」だといわれることが多い。地下鉄の中で話をすることもないし、目を合わせることさえない。ただしそれは愛想が悪いということではなく、イギリス人は他人のプライバシーをとても尊重するので、人が考えごとをしているときには話しかけないのだといわれる（そういえばアメリカ人は、ぼくが本を読もうとしているときに話を始めるので、うっとうしいことがあった）。

　しかしイギリス人は、人に話しかけたり助けたりするはっきりした理由があるときは、すぐ行動に移す。ぼくは最近、経済協力開発機構（OECD）がイギリスを「社会に貢献する姿勢」（簡単に言えば、人助けの精神だ）を持つ世界のベスト５カ国に入れたことを知った。ある新聞がこの評価を確かめるために、記者を取材に出した。たとえば若い女性記者に重いスーツケースを持たせ、急な階段の下で困っているふりをさせた。すると、ありとあらゆる人たちが助けに駆けつけた。なかには逆方向に歩いてい

たのに、走って戻ってきた人もいた。

　自分がけがをする前にこの記事を読んでいたら、ぼくはみんなが助けに来たのは「おとり」になった記者が若くてきれいな女性だったからだなどと皮肉な見方をしていただろう。でも、みんながぼくにも一生懸命に手を貸そうとしてくれたことを、今は自分自身の経験から知っている。イギリス人は無愛想にも見えるが、そんな見かけの裏側にとても親切な一面を秘めていることを、このけがのおかげで知ることができた。

2

イギリスらしさが詰まった小瓶

　このあいだ、ぼくは本当に「イギリス人らしい」ものとは何だろうと考えてみた。この国で生まれ育った人にしか当てはまらないものとは何だろうか、と。サッカーへの愛は、たいていのイギリス人男性が持っている（でも考えてみたら、ドイツ人男性もそうだ）。たいていのイギリス人は、お茶を飲むのが好きだ（でも、アイルランド人もそうだ）。イギリス人はきちんと列をつくるのが得意だ（でも、日本人もそうだ）。そんな具合。いろいろ考えたすえ、ぼくは「イギリス人らしさ」とはいくつかの特徴が混ざったもので、「この特徴はイギリス人すべてに当てはまる」とか「この特徴があるのはイギリス人だけだ」ということではないのだと理解した。

　それでもひとつだけ、これぞイギリスらしいと言えるものがあった。「マーマイト」という食べ物だ。イギリス人であれば、人生のいずれかの段階でマーマイトを口にしたことがあり、たいてい何か強烈なものを感じたと言って差しつかえないだろう。マーマイトについては有名な言葉がある。「愛するか憎むかのどちらか」。とはいえ外国の人は、マーマイトのことをほとんど聞いたこともないだろう。例外はイギリスでホームステイをしたことがある人だ。

イギリスのたいていの家庭には、マーマイトがひと瓶、必ず置かれている。

マーマイトがどんなものかを説明するのはむずかしい。ベタベタしていて、色は黒に近いペーストで、小さな瓶で売られている。あまり魅力的には見えないし、一部の人に言わせれば実際に口にしてみてそんなにおいしいものではない。ぼくがその味を描写するとしたら、「マーマイトっぽい」と言うだろう。あまりにも独特だからだ。さらに突っ込まれたら、ちょっと塩辛くて、ネバネバしているとつけ加えると思う。イギリス人なら誰でも、マーマイトはイースト抽出物でできていることを知っている。でもイースト抽出物とは何かと聞けば、多くのイギリス人が「それはマーマイトを作っているものだ」と答えるだろう。ぼくが知るかぎり、マーマイトを食べる方法はひとつしかない。トーストに薄く塗るのだ。

しかしマーマイトは、単なる食品の域を超えた存在になっている。イギリス人としてのアイデンティティーに、どこか結びついているのだ。おかしな話に聞こえると思うが、イギリス人は実際に食べることはほとんどなくても、マーマイトの瓶を家に置いておくことを愛国的な義務ととらえているようだ。海外に住んでいたときのぼくが、まさにそうだった。日本やアメリカからイギリスに帰るたびにマーマイトを買うのを忘れないようにしていたが、瓶を開

けて1度か2度食べたら、それきり戸棚にしまい込んでいた（ときどき、ほとんど触ってもいない瓶があるのを忘れて、新しいものを買ってしまうこともあった）。

　オーストラリアには「ベジマイト」という食品があって、マーマイトにとてもよく似ている。でも、オーストラリア人にはそう言わないほうがいい。イギリス人がマーマイトをひいきにする以上に、オーストラリア人はベジマイトのことが好きだからだ。愛国的なオーストラリア人はベジマイトのほうがマーマイトよりおいしいと主張するが、それはいずれにしても地味なグレーの色のなかで、ミリタリー・グレーがオーシャン・グレーよりすてきだと言っているようなものだ。

　2011年に、イギリス中を駆けめぐったニュースがあった。みんながメールで伝え合い、いくつものニュースサイトで「最も読まれている記事」の上位に入った。タイトルは「デンマークがマーマイトを禁止」。この記事は怒りと混乱の両方を同じくらい引き起こした。イギリス人は「そんなことをしていいのか？」と追及すべきか、「いったいなぜ？」と問いただすべきなのかわからなかった。ある新聞記事は、マーマイトを禁止すれば、デンマークは外国人の熟練労働者を引き止めにくくなるとまで書いた（マーマイトがなくなったら、イギリス人の専門職がこぞって母国に帰ってしまうとでも言いたげだった）。

実はデンマークが禁止しているのはマーマイトだけでなく、ビタミンを追加した栄養強化食品なのだが、イギリス人は国の誇りを傷つけられたかのように受け取った。これは不思議だった。マーマイトを頻繁に食べるイギリス人は10人に1人もいないからだ。それでもマーマイトは、イギリス人の意識のなかに大きな位置を占めている。イギリス人はたとえば、「ジョンはマーマイトみたいな男だ」などと言うかもしれない。それを聞いた人は「愛されるか憎まれるかのどちらか」の男なのだな、とわかるだろう。

3

愛されないぼくの故郷

「ぼくはエセックス生まれの男で、『エセックス男』じゃない」

このフレーズは、ぼくが90年代初めにひねり出して、ずいぶん使ったものだ。言いたかったのは、ぼくはエセックス州で生まれ育ったけれど、それがぼくという人間のすべてではないということだ。

ぼくはこの表現を2010年まで忘れていた。この年にぼくはイギリスに戻り、気がつけば、出身地を聞かれても「イギリスです」とか「ロンドンのあたりです」とは答えられなくなった。イギリス人相手には、エセックス出身と答えなくてはならなかったのだが、ぼくは「エセックス出身者」とくくられるのがあまり愉快ではなかった。

エセックスはイギリス中を見渡しても、いちばんイケてない地域だろう。おまけに、ぼくの育ったロムフォードは、そのエセックスの中でも、いちばんイケてない町かもしれない。ぼくはロムフォード生まれであることを恥ずかしいとは思わない。むしろ、とても好きな場所だし、行くのが楽しみな町だ（友だちがたくさんいて、家族が今も住んでいるということを差し引いても）。けれども厄介なのは、「エセックス出身」というだけで、まわりの人たちにある

種の色めがねで見られることだ。

　ある意味、エセックスは埼玉に似ている。すぐ近くにある首都に比べると、退屈な場所に思える。同じくロンドンに近いケント州のように風景の美しさで知られているわけでもなく、サリー州のように裕福な印象があるわけでもない。アメリカだとエセックスに似ているのはニュージャージー州で、どちらも文化の香りがしないというイメージがある。多くの人がいだいているエセックスのイメージは、階級が下の男たちがひどい英語を話し、汚い言葉を吐き、酒をたんまり飲んで、すぐにけんかをするといったようなことだ。女性はといえば、けばけばしいファッションが好きで、アルコールをかなり飲み、性的にも分別がないというイメージがある。エセックス出身の男性も女性も、きちんとした教育を受けておらず、お金を手に入れることと見栄を張ることにとりつかれていると思われている。

　こんな紋切り型のイメージは、ぼくが若かった90年代初めにあった。「エセックス女」についてはたくさんのジョークがあるし、「エセックス男」は元首相のマーガレット・サッチャーを尊敬する労働者階級の男性を意味した（エセックス男は社会の幸福より、金儲けに関心があるといわれていたためだ）。当時のイメージでは、エセックスの出身者は「粗野」で、けっこう恥ずかしい行いをした。男はみんな「ガズ」と呼ばれ、車をやたらとぶっ飛ば

し、白い靴下をはいていた。女の子はみんなシャロンだとかトレイシーという名前で、ジュエリーをじゃらじゃらいわせ、ナイトクラブではなぜかハンドバッグを真ん中に置いて、まったくイケてないダンスを踊っていた。

　外国に住んでいた間にこういう評判が消え去っていることを、ぼくは願っていた。ところが逆に、いっそうひどくなったように思える。その原因のひとつはテレビ番組だ。『ジ・オンリー・ウェイ・イズ・エセックス』という人気テレビドラマがあって、いかにもエセックス出身者にいそうな若者のライフスタイルを描いている。でもぼくはさらに運の悪いことに、最近ある「ドキュメンタリー」を見た。夜中にタクシーに乗ったロムフォードの人たちを、こっそり撮影したものだ。たいていは夜遊びから帰ってくる人たちだから、振る舞いも話し方も酔っ払いそのものだった。別のテレビ番組は、脱色したブロンドの髪で、ものすごく日焼けをして、夢は「サッカー・プレミアリーグの選手と結婚すること」というロムフォードの女の子の話をやっていた。番組ではこの女の子をスリランカの厳格な家庭に送り、親の厳しいしつけを経験させ、彼女の視野を広げさせた（見ていてけっこうつらかった）。

　ロムフォードの出身という理由だけで、イギリス人がぼくのことを無知だと思うのがどうして嫌なのか、読者のみなさんにはわかっていただけると思う。けれども、エセッ

クスが笑えるような人ばかりのひどい場所だという決めつけが消えないなかで、ぼくだけが知的だと認めてほしいわけではない。

　エセックスには教育や文化、あるいは正しい英語を話すことについて関心を持つ人がほとんどいないという事実に、ぼくは異論を唱えようと思わない。エセックスの多くの若者が酒をたくさん飲み、服や車にお金をたくさん使っているのを、ぼくは知っている。でも重要なのは、これがエセックス出身者だけでなく、今のイギリス全体の特徴だということだ。こういう恥ずかしい傾向がエセックスだけのものだと思えば安心できるかもしれないが、実はイギリス全体がかかえる問題なのだ。まともに考えれば、たとえばバッキンガムシャー州よりエセックスにこういう特徴が少しだけ強かったとしても、たいした話ではない。

　そこでぼくは、誰かがぼくのことを「エセックス男」と分類しようとしていると感じたときの答えを変えることに決めた。次は「ぼくはエセックス出身です。あなたもそうでしょ」と言おう。

4

イギリス式住宅購入術

 2012年の1月、ぼくは今までの人生で最大の変化ともいえそうな経験をした。家の持ち主になったのだ。たっぷり1年以上にわたり、物件を探す作業と購入にいたる細かな手続きがぼくの生活を支配した。そんなわけで、読者のみなさんには、なぜぼくがそのときの経験を披露したくなったかをご理解いただけると思う。

 ときにイギリス人は、引っ越しは人生で3番目にストレスの多い出来事だと言う（離婚と、配偶者との死別の次だ）。まわりの話を聞くと、ぼくの場合はわりとすんなり運んだほうだったようだ。それでもぼくは、今まで知らなかった技能をひととおり学ばなくてはいけなかったし、初めから終わりまで適切な「演技」をすることに集中しなくてはならなかった。

 まず、関心のある家の内見を手配する。けっこう多くの場合、まだその家に住んでいる所有者自身が案内してくれる。見も知らぬ人の家に入るのはとてもおかしな感じがするが、もっと奇妙なのはふだんなら守るべき礼儀を無視しなくてはいけないこと、そして内見する家について少しだけ否定的な態度をとらなくてはならないことだ（「あ、この部屋はちょっと暗いんですね……」）。その家がとても

気に入っているという態度を見せてはいけないし、できれば売り主には最近の景気の厳しさを思い出させたい。これらはすべて必要なことだ。というのも、もうこのときから実質的には価格交渉のプロセスが始まっているからだ。実際、本当にその物件が気に入って買いたいと思っているなら、関心のないふりをすることはとても重要になる。

買い手はどこかで妥協しなくてはならない。立地を第一に考える人もいるし、ガーデンがないと嫌だという人もいる。家に最新の設備があることを優先する人もいるだろう。大金持ちでもないかぎり、そのすべてがかなう家は手に入らないから、本当に欲しいものとそうでもないものを整理して考えなくてはいけない。

物件の売り主はいつも「売却希望価格」を出している。でも、その金額を本当に払ってはだめだ。ありえないほど高く設定されているからだ。買い手は、その価格よりかなり低い額の「オファー」を出さなくてはいけない。実際に払う用意のある額を最初からオファーすればいいと思うかもしれないが、オファーの額はもっと低くしないといけない。売り主は最初のオファーをほぼ必ず断ってくるからだ。そのあとで買い手は「最終オファー」をするかどうか、そこでどれだけ金額を積み上げるかを決めなくてはならない。

買い手としては、よけいな金を払いたくないという思いと、気に入った物件をわずかな金を惜しんだせいで逃し

たくないという気持ちの間で迷いに迷う。ぼくの場合は、売り主が価格をあまり下げなかったために、とても気に入った家をあきらめることになった。気持ちの面ではむずかしい決断だったが、金銭面を考えればあれでよかった。

売買価格に合意したあとにも、建築士に物件を調査してもらわないといけない。イギリスのほとんどの家は新築ではないし、古い家には目に見えない問題がありがちだからだ（最も深刻なのは地盤沈下、最も多いのは湿気に関するトラブル）。問題が見つかったら、買い手は売り主にまた値下げを頼むべきだ。けれども、これがなかなかむずかしい。誰だってお金の話をいつまでも続けたがる人はほとんどいないし、すでに売り主がかなりの値下げに応じていればなおさらのことだ。

これらの手続きを正しく行うことが重要なのは、イギリスの住宅価格が非常に高く、しっかり交渉すれば金額が相当に変わることがあるためだ。1997〜2007年に住宅価格は実に250パーセント上昇し、それ以降もほとんど下がっていない。ぼくの推計では、イギリス南東部の平均的な住宅価格は平均年収の7倍だ。家を買いたければ、身のすくむような額を借りなくてはならない。その一方で、イギリスでは住宅の資産価値が長期的には上がる。きちんと手入れをすれば、その可能性はさらに高まる。この点は、マンションの価値が20〜30年でなくなる日本とは大

きく違う。

　ぼくがいちばんストレスを感じたのは、最初の内見から契約を結ぶまで、とても時間がかかること（ふつう3〜6カ月かかる）、そしてその間なら売り主も買い手も理由に関係なく交渉を降りることができるということだ。売り主がもっといいオファーをもらうかもしれないし、仕事を失うかもしれないし、病気になるかもしれないし、物件を売ったあとの引っ越し先が見つからないかもしれない……。こんなことをあれこれ考えて眠れなくなった夜もある。

　これから1年半の間に住宅価格は少し下がるだろうと、ぼくは実は思っている。家を買うのはもう少し待つべきだったのかもしれないが、この決断は経済面だけでなく、自分のライフスタイルにもかかわるものだ。偉大な経済学者J・M・ケインズがかつて言ったように、「われわれは長期的には、みんな死んでいる」のだから。

　イギリス人は家を持つことに独特の強迫観念を持っている。ぼくも例外ではない。それでもぼくは、家を持つことでこんなにも誇りと満足が得られるのかと驚いた。実際、たいした家ではないかもしれない（立地が抜群なわけでもなく、少し暗いし、湿気も多く、大がかりな改装作業も必要だ）。でもぼくは、ビクトリア朝時代の小さな家とガーデンが自分のものであることを知っていて、そこに帰る。いい気分だ。

5

欲求不満への旅

　イギリスに住んでいて何にいちばんイライラするかと聞かれたら、ぼくは電車だと答えるだろう。イギリスの電車はあまり当てにならないし、料金は非常に高く、ばかばかしいくらいわかりにくい。

　たとえばコルチェスター駅でロンドンへ行く切符を買うと（ロンドンは約90キロ離れているから、だいたい小田原から東京くらいの距離）、朝と夕方のラッシュアワー以外はたいてい23.80ポンドだ。ところが同じ切符を日にちと電車を決めて少し前に予約すると、おそらく10ポンドですみ、場合によっては5ポンドですむ。ただし前売りの切符を買ったあとに予定が変わっても、乗る電車は替えられず、払い戻しも受けられない。

　イギリスの電車の切符にはたくさんの種類があって、納得のいくものもあれば、わけがわからないものもある。朝のラッシュアワーの電車がほかの時間より高いのは、それなりに理屈が通っているだろう。しかし往復切符を買っても、片道切符よりほんの少し高いだけだ（23.90ポンド）。「トラベルカード」という切符もあって、ロンドンの地下鉄とバスの1日乗り放題がついているのだが、この料金もたいていは往復切符よりわずかに高いだけだ（29.60ポン

ド)。何もついていない往復切符は、出かけた日と同じ日に帰ってこないといけない。ロンドンに行って翌日帰ってきたいときは、別の切符が必要になる(「オープン・リターン」というもっと高い切符で34.10ポンド)。

　切符の買い方を失敗してしまうのはよくあることだが、鉄道会社はそういう客にやさしくない。たとえば昼の12時30分にコルチェスターを出るロンドン行きの急行の前売り切符を買っていたのに、乗り遅れてしまったとする。そのため12時45分発の各駅停車に乗ったとして、もし車掌に見つかったら罰金を取られる。最初の切符に払った10ポンドは戻ってこないし、1本遅い電車の料金23.80ポンドを取られる。そのうえ23.80ポンドを罰金として取られる(合計57.60ポンドだ)。前売り切符を買っておいた電車が大幅に遅れたため、それより先に来た電車に乗った場合にも罰金を取られる(電車が遅れたのは鉄道会社のせいなのだが)。こういうことがあるので、前売り切符を使うのはとてもストレスがたまる。だから買わないようにしているという人もいる。

　イギリスに住む人たちは、もちろんこの国の電車のシステムが好きではないが、少なくとも慣れるチャンスはある。ぼくは予定が本当にはっきりしているときには前売り切符を買うし、ロンドンやその周辺に同じ日に行って帰ってくると片道切符に比べれば(あくまで「比べれば」だけ

ど）安くすむことも知っている。だからぼくは、何回もロンドンに行くより、いろんな用事を一日に詰め込むようにしている。このシステムをうまく使いこなす機会がほとんどない観光客や、ほかから来られる人たちには申し訳ないと思う。

　このあいだぼくは、イギリスに住む人なら誰もがいつかは遭遇する悪夢のような旅を体験した。ぼくはイースト・ロンドンのハックニーからロンドン西部の郊外リッチモンドに行こうとしていた。荷物が多かったから、時間はかかっても乗り換えのない経路で行くことにした。念のため前の日のうちに、ぼくは自分の乗りたい電車がその週末に通常どおり運行されるかどうかロンドンの交通局の人に尋ねた。彼はロンドン中のたくさんの「運行予定変更」を示す複雑な地図を見ていたが、ぼくが乗る予定の電車はいつもどおり走ると教えてくれた。

　彼はまちがっていた。ハックニー駅に行くと、ぼくが乗ろうとしていた電車がその日は途中までしか運行されず、そこで「代行バス」（イギリス人が大嫌いな言葉だ）に乗り換えなくてはいけないことがわかった。電車が止まったところには、バス乗り場への案内がなかった。ようやくバス乗り場を見つけたが、バスがそこに待っているわけでもない。ぼくたちは風と寒さの中、20分ほど待たなくてはならなかった。

バスはやって来たが、リッチモンドまで行くわけではないことがわかった。バスはのろのろと数キロ走り（残りの道のりのまだ半分くらいだ）、リッチモンドへ行く電車が出る地下鉄駅で乗客を降ろした。ぼくは重い荷物を抱えて階段を何度も上り下りしたから、もちろん相当にイライラしていた。そんなときには悪いことが重なるもので、目的地までほんのわずかの距離を走る地下鉄が到着するまで、さらに15分待たなくてはならなかった。1時間ですむと思っていた道のりが、ほぼ2倍かかってしまった。

切符のことも心配になった。ぼくは全区間の運賃を払っていたが、電車が途中で止まったとき、駅を出るために切符を使う必要があった。理屈からいえば、ぼくは残りの区間に有効な切符を持っておらず、ロンドンでは切符を持たずに電車に乗ると50ポンドの罰金を取られる可能性がある。ぼくは罰金を取られなかったが、乗客のなかには大事を取って運賃を2回払った人もいたと思う。

イギリスの公共交通機関は、乗客が目的地に着きさえすれば自分たちは役目を果たしたと思っているようだ。そこでぼくは、こんな広告コピーを思いついた。「イギリスの電車——料金は高く、ストレスもたっぷりに、あなたの行きたいところへ最後にはお連れします」

6

真珠のボタンは、誇りのボタン

　2012年のロンドン・オリンピックの前に、ぼくはイースト・ロンドンをずいぶん探索した。ぼく自身、ロンドンの東の郊外で育ったのだが、「イースト・エンド」と呼ばれる地域にはあまり行ったことがなかった。ロンドンに行くときにはそのあたりは通り越し、中心部や西部に行っていた。ぼくが特別なわけではない。ロンドンに来る人は、たいてい同じような場所に行っている。この街の名所の大半は、中心部から西部にある。国会議事堂、セントポール大聖堂、バッキンガム宮殿、ナショナル・ギャラリー、大英博物館、劇場街、有名な数々の店……。

　でも、ぼくはイースト・ロンドンもなかなかすてきな場所だと思うようになった。それはオリンピック・パークができたからではない。イースト・ロンドンには、この地域を独特なものにしている歴史と文化がある。ひとつ小さなことを取り上げると、「パーリー・キング」「パーリー・クイーン」の伝統が生まれたのはイースト・ロンドンだ。ぼくはこの伝統のことを最近までよく知らなかったが、実際に何人かのパーリー・クイーンに会って話を聞いたら、がぜん興味を持ってしまい、彼ら彼女らについて学ぶことになった。

イースト・ロンドンは昔から労働者階級が住む地域で、「パーリー」というのは労働者階級のなかの貴族のような存在だ。もしパーリー・キングを見たら、二度と忘れられないだろう。キラキラした多くのボタンできれいに飾られている黒いスーツと帽子を身につけている。スーツはかなり重い（おまけに夏は暑くて、冬は寒いのだそうだ）。ボタンは貝の「真珠層」と呼ばれる部分を使ったもので、いろいろな模様やモチーフを描いている（馬蹄は幸運を表し、いかりは希望を象徴する……といった具合だ）。パーリー・クイーンは色とりどりの羽のついた帽子をかぶっているから、その姿はもっと印象的だ。

パーリーにいちばん会えるのは、おめでたい行事のときだ。今年（2012年）は「別のクイーン」のダイヤモンド・ジュビリー（在位60周年）を記念する街角でのパーティーやお祭りがたくさんあるから、彼女たちはとても忙しい。パーリーたちはときどき歌うこともある（イースト・ロンドンにちなんだ歌で、みんなで歌えるものもいくつかある）。みんなパーリーたちの写真を撮りたがり、一緒に写真に入りたがる。パーリーたちはこれらをチャリティーの募金をつのるためにやっているのだが、同時に人々を元気づけてもいる。

この伝統は1870年代に、ヘンリー・クロフトという街路清掃人（孤児だった）がひょんなことからつくり出した。

伝えられるところによれば1860年代、日本からロンドンに、わりと安い値段の「真珠ボタン」が大量に届いた。ロンドンの街で野菜や果物を売る行商人たち（「コスターモンガー」と呼ばれる）が目立とうとして、このボタンを身につけるようになった。あたかもそれは、自分たちは本物の真珠をつけている金持ちのご婦人と平等なのだと言っているかのようだった。

クロフトはこのボタンを集めはじめ（通りを掃除しているときに見つけることがあった）、ジャケットに縫い込んだ。ある日、何百個ものボタンをつけて仕上げたスーツを着て、通りに立ち、「すべてチャリティーのため」に寄付をつのった。ぼくはこの話を聞いて、自分自身がとても貧しいのに他人のためにそんな努力をする人がいることに心を打たれた。当時の人々も心を打たれた。コスターモンガーたちが彼に加わりはじめ、自分のスーツを飾り立て、貧しい人たちのために寄付をつのったのだ。

クロフトが1930年にこの世を去ったとき、葬儀には約400人のパーリーたちが集まった。現在のパーリーは、そのころの「第1世代」のパーリーの子孫だ。パーリーというのは世襲の地位だからだ。パーリーの王女や王子もいて、7代目という人たちもいる。

イースト・ロンドンは急激な変化の中にある。イギリスの労働者階級にとって安住の地だった場所は、移民に

とっても最初の安住の地になっている。この地域には高級志向の再開発の波も押し寄せ、若い建築家やアーティスト、グラフィックデザイナーなどが住むようになった。昔のトゥルーマン・ビール醸造所や、果物や野菜を扱っていたスピタルフィールズ・マーケットに、今はギャラリーやブティックが軒を連ね、桶屋(おけ)や運搬人よりアーティストやファッション関係者が雇われている。ロンドンっ子のなかにはパーリーを、時代遅れのおかしな存在とみなす人もいる。でもぼくは彼らを、気持ちを前向きにしてくれる人たちだと思った。クロフト氏が意図したように、パーリーは希望と慈善の象徴であるとともに、移り変わりの激しい今の世界で変わらないものの象徴でもある。

7

ロンドン・スラング小辞典

　ふつうの英語ではないが、ロンドンではよく使われる言葉や表現がある。そのほんの一部を書き出してみた。

Bee's knees（表現）
the best（最高）という意味だが、少しだけ相手をばかにした否定的なニュアンスで使われることが多い。いわれはよくわからないが、音が似ていて、似た意味も持つ the business が元になっているのかもしれない。
［例文］He spent lots of money on a new suit and now he thinks he's the bee's knees.（あいつ、大金を出して新しいスーツ買ってさ、今は自分がいちばん格好いいって思ってるよ）

Bird（名詞）
ガールフレンド、あるいは女性。性差別的だとして、いい顔をされなくなってきた言葉だが、男性の友人同士では今もかなり使われている。女性は鳥のようにかわいらしくて快活で、（男性に比べると）小柄だという意味合いから。
［例文］I usually go out with my mates on Friday night but spend Saturday with my bird.（金曜の夜はたいてい男友だちと出歩くけど、土曜日は彼女と過ごすよ）

Boozer（名詞）

パブ。アルコールを意味する booze から。

［例文］We got kicked out of that boozer once for being too noisy.（あそこのパブ、一度騒ぎすぎて追い出されたことがあるんだ）

Brickie（名詞）

れんが職人（bricklayer）。ロンドンっ子がある種の職業を気軽なニックネームで呼んでいる例。ほかにも postie（postman＝郵便配達人）、sparky（electrician＝電気技師）、squaddie（soldier＝軍人）などがある。

［例文］Brickies have to work hard but there's good money in it.（れんが職人って大変そうだけど、けっこういいお金もらえるんだよね）

Cheers（表現）

「乾杯」という意味のほかに、thank you（ありがとう）、あるいは goodbye（さようなら）の意味で使われることがある。cheerio とまちがえないように。こちらは goodbye の意味はあるが、thank you の意味はない。

［例文］John told me that you sorted out the tickets for the game. Cheers, I really appreciate it.（ジョンに聞いたけど、試合のチケットを押さえてくれたんだって？ありがとう、感謝するよ）

Gaff（名詞）

家、あるいは住んでいる場所。いわれは不明。

［例文］Do you want to come round my gaff after the pub? I've recorded *Match of the Day*.（パブで飲んだあと、うちに寄る？ 『マッチ・オブ・ザ・デイ』〔BBCのサッカー番組〕を録画してあるよ）

Geezer（名詞）

男性。アメリカ英語では old man（老人）の意味になり、否定的な意味合いがあるが、イギリス英語では中立的な意味。ときどき diamond geezer（「頼れる友だち」「いいやつ」）というフレーズで使われる。よく似た用法の言葉に bloke があり、やや古い例では chap や fellow がある。

［例文］I saw your ex-bird with some geezer last night. Best to forget her.（ゆうべ、おまえの元カノが男と一緒にいるのを見たよ。もう忘れたほうがいいな）

Go pear shaped（表現）

物事が悪い方向に進む。たいていは予期しなかった状況について使う。

［例文］It was a good evening until someone suggested we have some tequila shots. After that everything went pear shaped.（このあいだの夜は最高だったんだけど、誰かがテキーラを飲もうって言い出して。そこからあ

とは大変なことになったよ)

Have a go（表現）
批判する、攻撃する。たいていは言葉によるものを指すが、ときに物理的なものを含む。似た表現に have a pop があり、こちらは物理的な攻撃を意味することが多い。
[例文] I made one little joke about his shirt and now he's telling everyone that I am always having a go at him.（シャツのことでちょっと冗談を言っただけなのに、あいつはぼくがいつも批判してくるって、みんなに言ってるんだ）

Have the hump（表現）
イライラする。たいていは人に対してだが、ときには状況についても使われる。イライラしたときに肩を上げ、あごを下げる姿勢が、背中に hump（こぶ）ができたように見えることから。
[例文] Why have you got the hump with me? I was only trying to help.（どうして私にイライラするわけ？ 手伝おうとしただけじゃない）

Plonker（名詞）
ばか。友だちを怒ったり、からかったりするときのやさしい表現。80年代にテレビ番組『オンリー・フールズ・アン

ド・ホーセズ』で広まった。似た意味で使われる語に wally がある。

[例文] I told Dave to take the 86 bus but he got the 68 and ended up in the middle of nowhere. What a plonker.（デイブに86番のバスに乗れって言ったのに、あいつ68番に乗っちゃって、わけわかんない場所に行ったんだって。ばかだよね）

See a man about a dog（表現）

「トイレに行く」の婉曲表現。使うのは男性だけで、たいていパブで使われる。その昔、人々はいらない子犬をパブに連れてきて、人に売ったりあげたりした。このためパブでちょっとだけ席をはずし、「犬の件で人に会いに行く」ことは珍しくなかった。これがトイレに行くことを意味する婉曲表現になった。

[例文] You get the beers in. I've got to see a man about a dog.（ビール、買ってきてくれる？　俺、トイレに行ってくるから）

Sprog（名詞）

子ども。ざっくばらんな、愛情のこもった表現。自分の子ども、あるいは友人・親戚の子どもを指すときに使う。かしこまった状況では使わず、よく知らない人の子どもついても使わない。古いドイツ語が由来。

［例文］My cousin had three sprogs before he was 25.（ぼくのいとこは、25歳でもう3人の子どもがいたよ）

Ta（表現）
thank you の最も省略された言い方。きちんとした感謝の言葉を述べるまでもない場合に、友人の間で使われる。ta very much とか ta muchly（こちらはおどけた言い方）と言えば意味が強まる。イングランド北部で goodbye の意味に使われる tara や ta-ta と混同しないように。
［例文］Pass me the milk, could you? Ta very much.（ミルクを取ってくれる？　ありがとう）

Take the Mickey（表現）
ばかにする、からかう。いつも人をからかっている人は Mickey-taker と呼ばれる。これに似ているが使用頻度の低い表現に extract the Michael がある。もっと下品で同じ意味の take the piss が由来。
［例文］He's always taking the Mickey. On Saturday he told me Arsenal lost 3-2 when actually they won 1-0.（あいつはいつも人をからかう。土曜日にはアーセナルが3－2で負けたって、ぼくに言ったんだ。本当は1－0で勝ったのに）

Wedge（名詞）

お金。ロンドンのスラングには folding stuff, dosh, wad などお金を意味する言葉がいろいろあるが、そのうちのひとつ。wedge は硬貨の一部分を指す古い英語。昔は少ない金額を示すために、硬貨を半分や4分の1にしていた。「給料」を指すこともある。

［例文］Pete's very mean with money. He gets good wedge but never spends any of it.（ピートって、本当にけちだよね。いい金もらってるのに、全然使わないもの）

Zilch（名詞）

「ゼロ」の意味を持つ、気軽だが強い言葉。もしかすると zero の最初の文字に、nil（これも「ゼロ」の意）の il がくっつき、音を強めるために ch が加えられたのかもしれない。さらに意味を強めたければ、a big fat zilch（大きくて太ったゼロ）とも言える。ロンドンっ子は同じような意味で absolutely nuffink（nuffink は nothing のくだけた言い方）という表現を使うこともある。

［例文］I put a charity collection box in my office last week. When I checked it today we had raised precisely zilch.（先週オフィスに募金箱を置いたんだけど、今日チェックしたら1ペニーも集まってなかったよ）

8

ときどきおかしな、秘密の言葉

　ぼくが地元出身の友だちと一緒にいるとき、とくに外国にいたり、外国人と一緒のとき、ぼくらにはイースト・ロンドン育ちの人間にしか使えない秘密の言葉のようなものがある。実際には「言葉」というほどのものではなく、方言の一部なのだが、人前で大きな声で話しても仲間にしかわからないことを口にできる。

　これは「コックニー・ライミング・スラング」と呼ばれるもので、イースト・ロンドンの労働者階級の人たちがよそ者にはわからないように話す暗号としてつくられた。ここでいう「よそ者」には警察官も含まれる（犯罪者もこのスラングを使っていたといわれている）。生まれたのは19世紀半ばで、それ以降、進化を続けてきた。

　いまコックニー・ライミング・スラングが使われることはいくらか減ったものの、以前よりはいくらか多くの人に理解されるようになった（辞書にも載っているし、インターネットでも調べられる）。イギリス人ならたいてい知っている核になる表現が20種類ほどあるのだが、外国人はいくら英語を上手に話す人でもほとんどわからない。

　コックニー・ライミング・スラングの「公式」は、簡単だとも複雑だともいえる。基本的にはなんらかの共通性の

あるふたつの単語の組み合わせを作り、2番目の単語と韻を踏む別の単語の意味に結びつける。よく知られている例をあげると、dog and bone（犬と骨）はphone（電話）の意味になり、jam jar（ジャムの瓶）はcar（車）のことになり、frog and toad（カエルとヒキガエル）はroad（道）の意味だ。一度覚えると簡単なのだが、初心者は"He drove a jam jar down the frog and toad."（彼はカエルとヒキガエルでジャムの瓶をドライブさせた＝道で車を運転した）と言われても、わけがわからないだろう。

もうひとつむずかしい点は、表現の後半部分が省略される場合が多いことだ。たとえば"Can I have a butcher's?"（「肉屋の」を貸してくれる？）と言われても、意味を推測する手立てがない。もし省略していないbutcher's hook（肉屋のフック）というフレーズを聞けば、lookの意味だとわかるかもしれない。つまり文全体では、"Can I have a look?"（見せてください）という意味になる。これに似た例には、hair（髪）の意味になるbarnetがある。19世紀のロンドンで有名だった馬の品評会Barnet Fairから来ている。

ときには、気づかないうちにライミング・スラングを使っていることもある。たとえば、ぼくはmoney（お金）の意味でbread（パン）と言っていたことがあるが、そのいわれがbread and honey（パンとハチミツ）にあるとは知ら

なかった。あるいは「考えてみろ」という意味で use your loaf という表現を使っていても、loaf が loaf of bread（パン1斤）の略で、つまり head（頭）を意味することを知らない人は多いと思う。

ぼくが好きな表現のなかには、特定の時代に生まれていても時を越えて生き残っているものがある。たとえば、誰かが「サッカーをやっていて Gregory を痛めた」と言うかもしれない。これは Gregory と言えば、誰もが俳優のグレゴリー・ペック（Gregory Peck）を思い浮かべた時代の表現で、Peck だから neck（首）の意味になる。今だったらパブで、"Get the Britneys in will you?"（ブリトニーズを買ってきてくれない？）と言う人がいるだろう。一瞬わからないかもしれないが、その場の状況を考えれば、ブリトニー・スピアーズ（Britney Spears）がビール（beers）の意味になっているとわかるはずだ。

最近のイギリスでは、若い人たちが話の中身を他人に知られたくないために、このスラングを使うようだ。たとえば "too many fridges"（冷蔵庫が多すぎる）と言えば、「このバーは男ばかりで、女の子が少なすぎる」ということだ。fridge freezer（冷凍冷蔵庫）が geezer（ロンドンの言葉で man のこと）の意味になる。あるいは "not sure about the boat race"（ボートレースのほうは微妙だ）と言えば、「この女の子はいい感じだけど、かわいくない」

ということだ。boat race が face の意味になる。

　ライミング・スラングは新しいものを即興で作ることもできるし、面白くて気の利いたものなら広まることもある。誰かが自然に新しいフレーズを作ったとき、ぼくはこのスラングがいちばん魅力を発揮すると思う。作るのも楽しいし、意味を「解読」するのも楽しい。ぼくの好きな即興スラングのひとつは、あごひげがもじゃもじゃの先生について友だちが言った "quite William and Mary"（かなりウィリアムとメアリー）というものだ。ウィリアムとメアリーはイングランドの共同統治者だったから、よく名前が一緒に出てくる。友だちはこれを hairy（毛むくじゃら）という意味で使ったのだ。

　別の例では、友だちがまだ赤ちゃんの息子を見て、"Oh no! He's done another Douglas."（やれやれ、この子、またダグラスをしちゃったよ）と言ったことがある。サッチャー時代の有名な政治家にダグラス・ハード（Douglas Hurd）という人がいた。友人はその名前を turd（うんち）の意味で使ったのだ。ぼくはすぐに意味がわかった。だからぼくたちは、臭いおむつを彼が替えなくてはいけないことがわかったとたん、一緒に楽しく笑うことができた。

9

国民的強迫観念

　150年ほど前、ロンドンのあるパブで非常に重要な会合が開かれた。いまぼくは「重要な」という言葉を少し迷いながら使った(歴史の大転換点というわけではなかったからだ)。だがそれ以降、この会合が数えきれないほどの人の生活に大きな影響を与えてきたことはまちがいない。

　1863年、フリーメイソンズ・タバーンというパブでフットボール協会(FA)が初めて会合を開き、サッカーのルールを整備しはじめた。この会合がパブで開かれたのは、とてもふさわしいことだった。以後、サッカーはパブで語られ、分析され、観戦されるようになったからだ。パブとサッカーの間には、持ちつ持たれつとも言えそうな関係がある。平均的なイギリス人男性は、ビールと「ザ・ゲーム」のふたつに夢中になる。ぼくの場合、今までで最高に幸せだった時間を思い起こすと、ビールを手にしてサッカーを見ていた瞬間がいくつか入るが、何もぼくが特別なわけではない。

　1863年以前には、イングランドにもほかの国にも、さまざまな種類のフットボールが存在した。しかし現在のサッカーがかたちを成しはじめたのは、このロンドンでの会合だった。最も重要な決定のひとつは「ハッキング」が許さ

れなくなったことだ。ボールを持っている選手を蹴ったり、ほかの方法でじゃまするのは反則とされることになった。もうひとつ大きな決定は、ボールを手に持って走るのを禁止したことだ。これがサッカーとラグビーが分かれる起源となった。長年の間にサッカーのルールは小幅の修正を施されたり、新しい規則が加えられたこともあったが、いま世界中で行われているサッカーが19世紀半ばにロンドンでつくられたルールを土台にしていることは明らかだ。

　サッカーはイギリスの「国民的娯楽」だ。あるスポーツジャーナリストが、イギリス人はふたつのスポーツに関心を持っているというジョークを言ったことがある。「サッカーと……その他」。イギリス人がみんなサッカーを好きだというわけではないが、まったく関心がなかったらまわりの話に入っていけないことが多くなるだろう。サッカーが好きではないと公言したら、多くの人から疎外されることになる（言いたいことが言えてすごいと思う人もいるだろうが）。ぼくは自分がサッカー嫌いだったらよかったのにと思うことがあるが、そうなるのは無理だと思う。サッカーは趣味として非常にお金がかかることがあるし、応援しているチームが負けるとつらくなることもある。選手がとんでもなく高い給料をもらっていながらチームに貢献していないようにみえると、腹立たしくもなる……。それでもぼくは、サッカーが見せてくれる筋書きのない「ドラ

マ」にとりつかれている。

　ときにサッカーは、イギリスの大衆にとって宗教のようにみえることがある。いうまでもなくイギリスでは、週末に教会へ行く人よりサッカーの試合を見る人のほうが多い。ファンが使う言葉にも宗教性を感じさせるものがある。すばらしい選手は「神」と呼ばれ、美しいゴールは「神々しい」と形容され、ファンは「チームはどの選手よりも大きな存在だ」と唱えたりする。自分が死んだら、好きなチームのピッチに遺灰をまいてほしいとファンが頼んでくるのも珍しいことではない。もちろんクラブはこういう依頼を断らざるをえないのだが、試合前に「長年のファンである○○氏が亡くなられました」などとアナウンスすることはある。

　ぼく自身はサッカーを重くとらえすぎないようにしている。試合を欠かさず見て、家族や仕事よりサッカーを大切にしている人（そういう人たちは本当にいるのだ）は、道を誤っている気がする。とはいえ、いろんなことがうまくいっていないときに自分のチームがすばらしい勝利を手にすると幸せな気分になれるし、逆にすてきな一日だったのにサポートしているチームがライバルに負けると一気に気分が悪くなる。ある友人がこんなふうに言ったことがある。「あっちじゃなくて、こっちのチームを応援しようという7歳のときの決断が、残りの人生の気分を左右するなん

ておかしいよな」

　その決断は予期せぬかたちで、自分のアイデンティティーに影響を与える。子どものころ、ぼくはたまたまアーセナルを応援することに決めた。アイルランド人の選手が多かったので、このチームは「ロンドンのアイルランド人」というぼくのアイデンティティーを象徴していると思ったのだ。けれども今のアーセナルにはアイルランド人の選手などおらず、むしろ「フランスのクラブ」になったなどといわれている（監督がフランス人で、選手もフランス人やフランス語圏出身者が多い）。昔のアーセナルは、わりと豊かで保守党を支持するロンドンの労働者階級のクラブだった（もともとは軍需工場で働く人たちがつくったクラブだったためだ）。

　ぼくたちはサッカーファンを独特の種族だと言うことがある。同じアーセナルのファンだとわかったために、友情が深まったこともある。イギリスではあいさつ代わりに「ゆうべの試合は見た？」とか、「あの新しい選手をどう思う？」と言うことがある。応援しているチームが勝てば、男同士で抱き合うこともある（日常生活ではめったにないことだ）。

　サッカーファンであるために生じる問題もある。友人のなかには、ぼくのクラブの古くからのライバルであるトッテナム・ホットスパー（スパーズ）のサポーターがいる。

このあいだ、ぼくの家に工務店の人が来たのだが、彼はリバプールのファンだと言った。ぼくは部屋に飾ってあったアーセナルの監督の写真を隠すことにした。それがもとで工務店の人がぼくのことを嫌いになり、いい加減な仕事をされたら困るからだ。

イギリス人男性はサッカーのことを驚くくらい率直に語ることがある。奥さんを愛していると公の場で口にしたことがなくても、サポートしているチームをどれだけ「愛している」かを語ることはある。ライバルチームを「憎んでいる」と言うこともある。

ある有名なサッカーの監督が冗談まじりにこんなことを言った。「サッカーは生きるか死ぬかの問題ではない。それよりも重要なことだ」。もちろんそんなことはないのだが、サッカーがこの国で大きな位置を占めていることはまちがいない。

10

１パイントのビールの買い方

　ぼくはイギリスに帰ってきたころ、イギリス人の自分にとって当たり前と思えることにも、実は独特の文化が詰まっていることを知った。たとえば、この国でビールを買うときには一定のルールと儀式があり、それらが外国から来た人にはわかりにくいことに気づいた。そればかりか、イギリス人にはこのルールがあまりに当たり前なので、わからない人に説明する必要があるなんて考えもしないことがある。そのくせ、この手続きに従わない人がいるとイライラしたりするのだ。そこでここでは、簡単そうにみえるこの作業の基本を少し解説してみたい。

　最初にやることは、当然ながらパブに入ること。これが思っているより少しだけ勇気がいる。パブの中は通りから見えないことがとても多いからだ（昔からパブの窓はすりガラスだった。客が妻や上司に見つからずに飲めるようにするためだ）。でも大きく息を吸って、中に入ってみよう。パブはイギリスで味わえるすばらしい経験のひとつなのだから。

　中に入ったら、誰かが出迎えたりテーブルへ案内してくれるのを、入り口のところに突っ立って待っていてはいけない。ウェイターはいない。好きなテーブルを見つけて、

そこに陣取ろう。でもテーブルに座ったまま、誰かが注文を取りに来るのを待ってはいけない。テーブルにメニューが置いてあってもだ。ビールを買うには、自分でカウンターに行って注文しなくてはならない。ロンドンでは観光客がテーブルに座ったまま、ほかの客がどうやってビールを買っているかがわかるまで、注文を取りに来るのをしばらく待っている光景をよく目にする。

カウンターのあたりには、きちんとした順番待ちの列がないようにみえる。客はカウンターの幅いっぱいに広がって立ち、注文を聞いてもらえるのを待っている。でも、秩序がないように見えるのは見かけだけだ。イギリスのパブには、おおざっぱだが機能的な順番待ちのシステムがある。客はほとんど無意識のうちに、誰が自分より先に待っていたか、誰が自分のあとに来たかを知っている。その順番を無視して注文するのは、まったく礼儀に反している。パブのスタッフは客が来た順番どおりに対応しようとするが、混み合ってきたらわからなくなってくる。そんなときスタッフは、客の「自主管理」に頼る。「次は誰?」と、彼らは聞く。もし次が自分の番なら、手を挙げるだけでいい。確信が持てなかったら、まわりの客に「そっちが先だったっけ?」と聞こう。

パブのスタッフをウェイターのように扱ってはいけない。指をパチンと鳴らして何かを頼もうとしたり、「注文した

いんですが」と言ったりしてはだめだ。スタッフに何かを頼みたいときは笑顔とアイコンタクトで注意を引いたほうがいいし、必要であれば畳んだ10ポンド紙幣を掲げて、ビールが欲しいという意思を伝えよう。スタッフもふつうは客を「サー」とは呼ばず、もっと気軽で打ち解けた話し方をしてくる。

　パブのスタッフに、じかにチップを渡してはいけない。ほとんどの人はチップを渡さないが、もし渡したくなっても現金はあげないほうがいい。その代わり、ビールを買うときに、彼らにおごりたいと言おう（「1杯飲んでよ」）。スタッフはきっと「ありがとう。あとでいただきます」と答え、あなたに払うおつりから1～2ポンドを取るだろう。だから実際は現金のチップなのだが、飲み物をおごったという体裁になっている。

　日本などの国のように、ただ「ビールください」と注文することはできない。いろいろなビールがあるから、選ばなくてはいけない。静かなパブなら、おすすめのビールを聞くのもいい。でも、街の真ん中にある混雑した店ではやめておこう。店のほうは、注文を早く決めてほしいと思っている。カウンターに並んでいるタップ（ビールサーバーの注ぎ口）を見回して適当に選ぶのもいいが、イギリスにはさまざまな種類のビールがある。ラガー、ビター、スタウト、サイダー……。飲みたいビールの種類がわかって

いるなら、「ラガーください」などと言おう。店のスタッフはラガーをそそいでくれるか、店で扱っているラガーの名を挙げて選べるようにしてくれるだろう。

とくに何も言わなければ、ビールは1パイントのグラスにそそがれる。昔からある568ミリリットルのイギリスのグラスだ。多いと思う人もいるようだが、イギリス人には標準サイズだ（イギリス人はこれを何杯も飲む）。ハーフパイントを頼むこともできるが、イギリス人はめったに注文しない。おかわりをするために何度もカウンターに行きたくないからだ。

パブで使われるわかりにくい表現がいくつかある。"What's your poison?"（あなたの毒は何？）は、"What would you like to drink?"（何を飲みますか？）のふざけた言い方だ。パブのスタッフが言ったり、あなたに飲み物をおごろうとしている人が言うかもしれない（アルコールはある種の毒なのだが、飲む人たちは「どんな毒を飲みたいか？」と互いに尋ねることで、その事実を重くとらえないようにしている）。

パブのスタッフに "Is that dead?"（死んでる？）と尋ねられることがあるかもしれない。これも驚かないように。スタッフが言いたいのは "Have you finished with that drink?"（そのグラスはもうすんだ？）ということだ。グラスの最後の一滴まできれいにしたい人もいるし、少し残

す人もいる。そこで、この独特の表現でグラスを下げていいかどうかを確かめる。

パブのもうひとつのキーワードは「ラウンド」だ。ビールを順番におごり合うシステムのことである。誰かが友だちみんなの分も払ったら、次の1杯は別の人が払い、また次の1杯は……というふうに続く。誰かが飲み物を買ってくれたら、次の1杯は "I believe it's my round."（今度はぼくの番だね）と言って、おごり返すのが礼儀だ。ここまでくれば、パブのマナー初級編は合格だ。

11

イングランドの歌

　イギリスが独特である点のなかに、ひとつの国家でありながら、複数の「国」から成り立っているということがある。イングランド、スコットランド、ウェールズ、北アイルランドはそれぞれアイデンティティーを持ち、スポーツの代表チームもあるから、ときにはイギリス人だけが出場する「国際試合」が行われる。たとえばラグビーではスコットランドとイングランドが戦っているし、サッカーでは北アイルランドとウェールズが対戦することもあるかもしれない。

　スポーツで国の代表が戦うとき、ふつうは試合前にそれぞれの国歌が流れる。だからイギリスのチームの場合は、ちょっとおかしなことになる。イギリス全体の国歌は「ゴッド・セイブ・ザ・クイーン」だが、スコットランドとウェールズには第二の国歌があって、そちらを使うこともできる。それぞれ「スコットランドの花」と「わが父祖の土地」だ。現在のところ、イングランドと北アイルランドは「ゴッド・セイブ・ザ・クイーン」を使っている。もしこの2チームが対戦したら、同じ国歌が2回流れるのかと思う人がときどきいる（実際には1回だけだ）。

　「スコットランドの花」は印象深く、歌いやすい曲で、

1314年に起きたイングランドとの戦いでのスコットランドの勝利を記念している。古い歌だと思われることもあるが、実は1967年に生まれたもので、ザ・コリーズというフォークバンドが作った。「わが父祖の土地」は感動的で、いつもウェールズ語で歌われる（だから正式な題名は「ヘン・ウラッド・ヴー・ナーダイ」という）。

　ここで声を大にして言いたいのは、ぼくはイングランド人としてうらやましく思うということだ。スコットランドとウェールズにはいわば「オーダーメイド」の力強い国歌があるのに、イングランドには相変わらず「ゴッド・セイブ・ザ・クイーン」しかない。ぼくはこの歌がそれほど好きではない。曲があまり面白くないし、イングランド人だけのものというわけでもない。詞もぼくにとっては、気持ちをかき立ててくれるものではない。ぼくが女王を嫌いだというわけではなく、女王をたたえる歌がイングランドのアイデンティティーを表現する最も適切なものだとは思えないのだ。こう考えているのは、ぼくだけではない。イングランドでも第二の国歌を選ぼうという議論がときどき起こっている。

　イングランド独自の国歌には「希望と栄光の国」がいいという人はけっこういる。確かにこの歌は力強く、よく知られている。イングランド人のエドワード・エルガーが作曲し、A・C・ベンソンが詞を書いている。問題はその詞

が、書かれた当時（1902年）のあからさまな帝国主義を反映しているということだ。まず、この詞はイギリスが帝国の版図を拡大させるよう訴える。「広大に、いっそう広大に／汝の土地はなるべし／神、汝を偉大たらしめし者が／いっそう汝を偉大にしますように」。だから、この歌は「好戦的愛国主義」にあふれており、今の時代にふさわしいとは思えない。

これに似た問題は、とても愛されている別の歌「我は汝に誓う、我が祖国よ」にもある。美しい旋律はグスターヴ・ホルストの「木星」（組曲「惑星」より）からとられ、歌詞はイギリス人外交官のセシル・スプリング・ライスの詩からとられている。問題なのは1番の歌詞だ。もうやみくもに愛国主義的なのだ。歌詞では、人は自分の国を無条件に愛し、国のためなら命も捧げよと訴える。この歌は最後の節でいくらか挽回していると思う。われわれが奉仕すべき「もうひとつの国」（神の国）があると唱えているからだ。

イングランドの国歌の最も有力な候補は、おそらく「エルサレム」だろう。大仰なメロディーに、ウィリアム・ブレイクの詩からとった歌詞がついている。ぼくが面白いと思うのは、この詩にはある種のあいまいさがあり、そのため別々の信条を持つ人たちもそれぞれに気に入っているという点だ。歌詞は、キリストはイングランドにやって来

たのかと問いかける(答えは詞の中にはない)。そして、イングランドをよりよい国にするという決意が表明される。右派の人たちはこの詞が好きだ。イングランドが神に愛された特別な国であることを示唆しているからだ。左派の人たちはこの歌を「新しいエルサレム」(もっと公正な社会)を築けという呼びかけととらえている。

　ほかにもいくつか、ちょっととっぴな候補が挙げられている。ラグビーファンは「スウィング・ロウ、スウィート・チャリオット」(試合中にファンが歌う歌だ)を推している。でも、ぼくはいいアイデアだと思わない。この歌はアフリカ系アメリカ人が19世紀に作った黒人霊歌であり、キリスト教の聖歌だから、イングランドに起源があるわけではない。おまけにラグビーファンにしか人気がない。サッカーファンは、自分たちが応援歌にしている曲のほうがいいと冗談半分で反論するかもしれない。映画『大脱走』のテーマだ。この映画は、第2次世界大戦中のドイツの捕虜収容所から連合軍の捕虜が脱走を企てるという話だ。曲はとても覚えやすくて明るいけれど、アメリカ人が作った映画のためにアメリカ人が書いたものだ。

　でもサッカーファンのアイデアは、けっこういいところを突いているのかもしれない。イングランド人が歌詞のない歌を選べば、いろいろな問題を避けられるのではないかとぼくは思うことがある。国歌には歌詞がないといけな

いわけではない（スペイン国歌には歌詞がない）。イングランドが考えてみてもいい候補は、エルガーの「エニグマ（謎）変奏曲」の中の「ニムロッド」だろう。謎めいていて、気持ちを高めてくれるこの曲は、追悼の場などで流れることが多い。詞がないので、誰もが自分の好きな意味合いを曲にのせられる。ぼくなら、この曲がイングランド人の静かな決意を表していると想像する。でもそれよりは、イングランドの風景が持つ繊細な美しさを描いていると思う人もいるだろう。つまり、自分たちが何者かという点で意見がそろうことのない国民の国歌としては、いい具合に「謎めいて」いるのではないだろうか。

12

ロンドンの「もうひとつ」の水路

　ロンドンでいちばん重要な水路はどれかと聞かれたら、ほとんど誰もがテムズ川だと答えるはずだ。でももうひとつ、魅力的な水路がある。リージェンツ運河だ。この運河はもっと知られていいはずだし、実際に今、ちょっとした「復活」の途上にある。

　リージェンツ運河が造られたのは19世紀初めのことで、ロンドンの物流を効率化するためだった。全長は14キロ近くあり、ロンドン西部のパディントンの近くから東部のライムハウスまで延びて、そこでテムズ川と合流する。物流業の主力が自動車と鉄道に移行すると、当然ながら運河はあまり使われなくなった。1960年代になると、運河は古い遺跡のようになった。

　そんな衰退の道をたどりながらも、リージェンツ運河はロンドンが誇るべきもののひとつだと、ぼくは思っている。そう思うようになったのはわりと最近で、運河を知ったのは2010年のことなのだが、それ以来ぼくはこの運河沿いをけっこう歩いている。午後を丸々つぶして端から端まで歩いたこともある。

　リージェンツ運河についてまず言っておきたいのは、テムズ川とはまるで違うということだ。テムズ川は幅の広い

感潮河川（潮の干満の影響で流速や水位が変わる河川）で、印象的な風景を持ち、立派な橋が架かっている。運河のほうは幅が狭く静かで、景色もあまりぱっとしないが、そういう点が魅力の一部になっている。運河沿いに行くと、ロンドンにいることを忘れそうになるだろう。ビルもあまり見えないし、車の音もほとんど聞こえない。

　リージェンツ運河についてもうひとつ大事なことは、イギリス中の運河と同じく、「引き船道」が運河沿いに設けられていることだ。昔は馬が運河沿いのこの道で荷船を引いていた。この点はベネチアや江戸時代の東京など、竿やオールで船を操っていたほかの多くの都市と違う。エンジンの発明によって引き船道はほとんど無用の存在になったが、幸いにも現在は、歩いたり自転車を走らせる人たちにとって最高の道になっている。

　これまで長いこと、引き船道を使うのは歩きたい人や犬を散歩させる人くらいだったかもしれない。でも今は、通勤のためにリージェンツ運河の引き船道を歩いたり自転車で走る人が増えているようだ。混雑していて料金も高いロンドンの公共交通機関を使うのに比べれば、はるかに快適だ。

　リージェンツ運河沿いには、人気のスポットがいくつもある。たとえば運河はカムデンを通る。有名な市場があるところで、屋台もたくさんある。ここで食べ物を買って、

運河沿いで食べるのが人気だ。あるいは、リトル・ベニスと呼ばれる地域もある。リージェンツ運河がグランド・ユニオン運河（200キロ以上も北のバーミンガムまで延びている）と交わる場所だ。リージェンツ運河はリトル・ベニスで、パディントン・ベイスンのほうへ分岐する。昔は船が係留されて積み荷を降ろしたところだ。そんなふうに、このあたりには水路が集まっていて、散歩をしたり静かに本を読んだりするのに絶好の場所になっている。

ただし、ぼくはカムデンもリトル・ベニスも好きだけれど、そこへ行っただけではリージェンツ運河の魅力を存分に味わえないと思う。おすすめしたいのは、やはり運河に沿って進んでみることだ。歩くにつれて景色が移り変わっていく。パディントン・ベイスンでは、オフィスや店舗、レストランが目立つ。ほかの場所だと緑が多く、木陰もある。カムデンを通り抜けるときは人がごった返しているが、何分かするとまたほとんど人がいなくなる。ぼくがとくに気に入っているのは、この運河がロンドン動物園を抜けるところだ。運河の一方には変わった鳥がいて、反対側にはハイエナがいる。イースト・ロンドンに入ると、運河沿いの地域にも工場の跡地などが見えて、ごつごつした風景になってくる。

もちろん、ぼくは運河を舟で行き来してみたいと思う。というより、運河はそのために造られている。古くからイ

ギリスの運河を行き来してきた細長い「ナロー・ボート」は、これまで造られた乗り物のなかでも指折りの美しさだ。昔ながらの塗装と装飾が施され、見た目が同じものはふたつとない。ぼくがとくに気に入っているのは、この舟が速さを求められていないことだ。最近は馬が引くのではなく、ディーゼルエンジンが積まれているが、それでも歩く速さとあまり変わらない。おまけに水門を通るときには、かなり時間がかかることもある。だからナロー・ボートの上では、のんびりしたペースに合わせないといけない。

　ナロー・ボートが好きな人は、ぼくのほかにもたくさんいるようだ。休暇に借り上げる人もいるし、イングランド中を旅するために買ってしまう人もいる。最近では住居としても人気を集めている。ロンドンの住宅価格が途方もなく高いため、ナロー・ボートを買ってロンドンのあちこちに停泊して暮らそうという人たちが現れてきた。ぼくの友人にもこれをやった男がいる。彼によれば大きな魅力のひとつは、仕事を変えたときや、単に目に映る風景を変えたくなったときに「引っ越し」が簡単にできるという点だ。

　物流の動脈としての役割を終えたあと、運河には存在意義がなくなったようにみえた時期があっただろう。でも今は、通勤や生活、あるいは娯楽に使われる貴重な財産になっている。リージェンツ運河はロンドンの歴史の一部というだけでなく、現在のロンドンの一部でもある。

13
天気の話をする

　イギリス人は天気の話をよくする。友だちに会ったときにまず天気の話をすることも多いし、知らない人と会話を始めるのに天気を話題にすることもよくある。一見してイギリス人は、天気について文句ばかり言っているようにみえるだろう。たとえば雨が降ってきたら、バスの停留所で隣にいる人に「またですね……」と、首を振りながら言うかもしれない。ピクニックを楽しんでいるときに強い風がいきなり吹いてきて何もかも吹き飛ばしたら、友だちに「なんで今日に限って風が吹くんだ」と言うかもしれない。

　でもぼくは、みんなが本当に文句を言っているわけではないと思っている。たいていの場合、彼らは互いに慰めあっており、なんとか今の状況を受け入れようとしていて、ひどい天気による不都合は少なくともみんなが共有していることを確認しあっているのだ。「この雨と寒さには本当にうんざりだ」というように、心の底から否定的な言い方をすることはあまりないだろう。

　イギリス人は天気をジョークのネタにもする。寒いときには友だちに「大丈夫？　ちゃんと寒い？」と言うこともある。もちろん、もっと寒くなってほしいとは誰も思っていないから、これはほんのジョークだ。あるいは曇りの日

に少しだけ太陽が出てきたら、「日光をほんの少し浴びる危険があるね」と言うかもしれない。これも太陽が見えてきたら危ないと感じるという、ちょっと冗談ぽい言い方になっている。

　イギリスでは毎年3月末に、時計の針を1時間進める。サマータイム（夏時間）の始まりだ（10～3月はグリニッジ標準時が使われている）。3月はまだ寒くて雨も多いので、サマータイムの始まりはイギリスでやたらとジョークのネタにされる。1週間かそこらは、みんな「これでもサマー？」と言っている。

　ぼくが面白いと思うのは、イギリスの天気はたいていとても穏やかなのに、なぜかイギリス人は天気の話をたくさんするということだ。ロンドンは、たとえばモスクワのようにめちゃくちゃ寒くはない。ハリケーンも来ないし、雨季もないし、湿度が高いわけでもない。イギリスの夏は夜が長くて明るくて、それほど暑くもなく、世界でも指折りのすてきな夏なのではないかと、ぼくは思っている。

　奇妙なことに、イギリス人が天気に文句を言うのは、暑すぎると思ったときだ。30度以上の気温が何日か続くと、イギリス人は「熱波」が来たと言う。みんな、この暑さの中で「しおれてしまう」などと言うだろう。こんな言葉を聞くと、ぼくはいつも笑い出しそうになる。東京やニューヨークがどれだけ暑くて、どれだけ湿気が多いかを知っ

ているからだ。

　この夏（2013年）もイギリスは「熱波」を経験し、ぼくはなぜイギリス人が暑さを嫌うのかがようやく少しわかった。イギリスは暑さにしっかり対処するようにできていないのだ。たとえば地下鉄のほとんどの電車や駅にはエアコンがなく、気が変になりそうなほど暑くなる。いずれにしてもイギリス人はエアコンに慣れていないから、使えるときでも（たとえば車に乗っているときとか）、窓を開けてエアコンの効果を台なしにしてしまう。イギリス人にしてみれば、車を涼しくしてくれるのは自然の風なのだ。

　こうした無知は今に始まったことではない。ビクトリア朝時代にはサッシ窓（上げ下げ窓）という原始的な「エアコン」があった。サッシ窓はこの時代に建てられたイギリスの家にはよくあるもので、上と下の両方から開けられる。暑い日には上の窓を途中まで下ろし、下の窓を途中まで上げる。こうすると空気の自然な循環をうまく使うことができて、暑い空気が窓の上から外へ逃げ、涼しい空気が窓の下から入ってくる。ところが残念なことに、多くの人がこの仕組みを理解せず、下の窓だけ開けている。もっとひどい場合には、ペンキをたっぷり使って窓を塗ってしまい、上下のどちらか一方からしか開かなくなっていることもある。

　イギリス人は暑さの中で体調をどう保っていくかも知ら

ない。のどが乾いたり、疲れて家に帰ってきたりしても、熱いお茶を飲むのがふつうだ。多くの人が真夏にも熱いお茶を飲んでいて、これが逆効果だということがわかっていない。イギリスで男性が暑い日に半ズボンとサンダル姿になることが受け入れられるようになったのも、ごく最近だ。ひと世代前だったら、男らしくないと思われていただろう。実はぼくもこの件については「守旧派」で、いくら暑くても街に出るときは半ズボンをはかない。

　このあいだ、悲しいけれどおかしな話を聞いた。ロンドンで新しいバスが導入され、快適なエアコンがついていたのだが、窓が開かないようになっていた。暑い日に乗客がわざわざ開けないようにするためだ。ところが外の気温がいつもより高いときにエアコンが壊れ、バスの中が30度以上になってしまった。バスはすぐに「移動式サウナ」と呼ばれるようになった。このフレーズは、不満と冗談を結びつけるイギリス人の才能を示していると思う。

14

偶然の庭師

 2年前、ぼくは家を買った。本当に買いたい家ではなかった(いちばん気に入った家は少し高すぎた)。でも家族や友人たちは、ぼくが買った家には小さな庭があるから、こっちのほうがずっとよかったと慰めてくれた。天気のいい日には庭で寝転がってもいいし、バーベキューもできるし、野菜だって育てられるじゃない……などと明るく言ってくれた。

 ぼく自身は、いいのかどうかよくわからなかった。それまで自分のガーデンを持ったことなんてなかったし、何度か観葉植物を家に置いたときでさえ水をやらなかったか、やりすぎたかのどちらかで見事に枯らしてしまった。だから自分のガーデンを持つなんて、最初から失敗に終わることがわかっている大事業のように思えてならなかった。

 思ったとおり、ぼくはそれ以来、失敗を重ねた。ルバーブを育てようと思ったのは、とても強い野菜で、あまり手間がかからないといわれていたからだ。ぼくはルバーブのパイが好きだし、そのパイを自分のガーデンから作る日を夢見ていた。ぼくはルバーブに数日おきに水を少しやり、すべて順調にみえたのだが、ガーデンに新しい物置を入れるときに踏んづけられてしまった。ハーブもいくつか

買ったのだけど、寒さと雪が続いたせいでやられてしまった（それも4月に！）。ガーデンを照らしていたソーラーライトは、もう何度も風に吹き飛ばされたり、さまざまな侵入者（人間も動物も）に壊されたりした。ぼくはハリネズミがガーデンに来てくれたらいいのにと心から思った。ハリネズミ1匹がすむのに理想的なスペースは作ってやれる。でもぼくの不運のせいでハリネズミが死んだりしたら、もう耐えられないと思った。

その一方で、ぼくが成功した部分もある（自分の手柄だとは言いきれないけれど）。たとえば今年（2013年）は、ガーデンの隅にあるリンゴの木に大きなリンゴがたくさんなった。家庭のガーデンにあるリンゴの木からは、たいてい「料理用リンゴ」しかとれない（すっぱすぎて砂糖を加えないと食べられないようなリンゴなので、パイかジャムにするしかない）。でも、わが家のリンゴはちょっとすっぱいけれど、問題なく食べられる。信じられないことに、ガーデンの目立たないところにある木がスモモだと今年になってわかり、夏にはおいしくて甘いスモモがいくらか収穫できた。茂みの中のあちこちでブラックベリーも育つので、8月から9月には朝食のときにこの3つの果物を合わせて食べていた。

イングリッシュ・ガーデンを本当にきれいに造るには、つねに注意を払わないといけない。ぼくは家を空けること

が多いので、なかなかちゃんと面倒を見られない。家にいるときでさえ、ガーデンの作業をせずに何週間も過ごしてしまうことがある。そんなふうに放っておくと、どんどん大きな顔をするようになる植物がある。グラス類がひざのあたりまで伸び、ブッドレアとハニーサックルがほかの植物のスペースに侵入しはじめる。ぼくはゆっくりとだが、家庭のガーデンのことを学んでいる。1年前だったらブッドレアなどという名前は知らなかっただろうし、この植物がチョウに好かれるので「バタフライ・ブッシュ」と呼ばれていることも知らなかったろう。ハニーサックルは蜂に好かれ、長いグラス類は猫に好かれることも知った。

　ガーデンを重荷に感じることもある。夏に伸びすぎた草木を刈り込むのは、面倒な作業になりかねない。今年の夏はとても暑くて乾燥していたので、夜中に庭に出て植物に少し水をやらないといけないと思ったものだ。それに、ぼくはよくナメクジやカタツムリ（庭師の敵だ）を踏んづけてしまうのだが、あればかりはずいぶん気持ちの悪い経験だ。それでもぼくは、自分のガーデンに少しずつ愛着を持つようになったようだ。たとえばある日気がつくと、ぼくはリンゴの木について書いた新聞記事を読んでいた（ぼくはリンゴを早く収穫しすぎていたことがわかった。6月が寒くて雨続きだったから、あと数週間待つべきだったのだ）。ガーデニングの本も買って、ときどき読んでい

る。ゴボウを育てようかとも考えた（日本で食べていたようなゴボウサラダを作りたかった）。でもイングランドではゴボウは「バードック」と呼ばれていて、面倒な雑草のような扱いをされていることがわかった。

　この原稿を書いているのは夜の早い時間だが、このくらいになるとクロウタドリが近くの木に止まり、歌声を聞かせてくれる。ぼくはこの家に引っ越すまでクロウタドリの歌声を聞いたことがなかったが、これほど美しく、落ち着いた気持ちにさせてくれるものはあまりないと思う。この鳥の声を聞くと、小さくて乱雑で管理もずさんだけれど、ガーデンのついたこの家を買えて幸運だったと思っている自分に気づく。

15

奇妙にイギリス人らしいエイリアン

　ぼくは先日、BBCの生放送番組を見ていた。この番組では、ある重要な地位を誰が受け継ぐかがわかるはずだった。といっても、政党の新しい指導者ではないし、政府機関のトップでもない。サッカーチームの新監督でもなかった。この番組で伝えられようとしていたのは、「ドクター・フー」と呼ばれるテレビドラマのキャラクターを次に演じる俳優だった。

　ぼくは不思議な感じがした。ドクター・フーは海外ではほとんど知られていないのに、イギリスではもうすぐ別の俳優が演じるという「ニュース」だけで番組が丸ごと作られるほど重要な存在なのだ。それまで何週間か、新聞は新しいドクター・フーは誰になるかという推測記事を載せていたし、評論家のなかには特定の俳優がふさわしい理由を解説する人たちまでいた。

　ここでドクター・フーについて説明しておいたほうがいいだろう。彼はBBCのドラマ（タイトルも『ドクター・フー』）の主人公だ。このドラマは、ぼくが生まれるずっと前に始まった。第1回は1963年で、これまで約800話が放映されている。「ザ・ドクター」（と彼はよく呼ばれる）は、時代と空間を一瞬のうちに行き来するタイムトラベ

ラーで、惑星を壊滅から救ったり、悪い異星人と戦ったりする。ガリフレイという惑星からやって来たことになっているが、彼はイギリスのアクセントで話し、イギリス人らしい性格をしている（たとえばユーモアのセンスや、ちょっと変人っぽいところだ）。いうなれば、彼はジェームズ・ボンドのSF版なのだ。

70年代に子ども時代を過ごしたぼくは、驚きと恐怖が入り混じった気持ちで『ドクター・フー』を毎週見ていた。本当に怖い回もあった。とくにドクターの戦う敵がダーレクのときだ。ダーレクは容赦ないほど邪悪な種族で、金属のシェルの中に入っている。自分に反抗する者を殺すときには機械的な声で「抹殺セヨ！ 抹殺セヨ！」と叫ぶ。ぼくを含め『ドクター・フー』を見ていた多くの子どもたちは、まさに（そのころ言われていたように）「ソファの陰からこわごわとのぞき見る」という感じだった。

もちろん、『ドクター・フー』の骨組みになっているアイデア自体はありふれたものだ。ほとんどの人がその存在を知らず、抵抗するすべもない危機が忍び寄る。そこへ勇敢で聡明なヒーローが戦うために現れる。彼は圧倒的に不利な状況に陥り、希望は絶たれるかにみえる。しかし最後に彼は勝利をつかみ、誰もが溜飲を下げる。ぼくたち視聴者は少し気持ちを晴らし、元気づけられる。

けれどもドクター・フーは、実にイギリス的なヒーロー

だ。彼の大きな特徴は、いつも弱い者を攻撃的ないじめっ子タイプから守ることだ。彼は自分が認められなくても別にかまわないし（彼が救う惑星の住人は、自分たちが危機に瀕していることを知らない場合が多い）、固い決意をいだいている。この意味でドクター・フーは、イギリス人が自分たちについて持っている自画像を体現した存在だ。

　彼はみんなをひとつにする存在でもある。イギリスで彼は、ほとんど誰にでも愛されている（それはたとえば、この国の政治指導者とは違う）。みんながいつも見ているとは限らないが、年齢や住んでいる場所を問わず、誰もがこの番組が好きだ。ぼくは最近、7歳の男の子とドクター・フーについて長いこと話したが、ふたりともその会話に同じくらいの関心を持っていた（あまりないことだ）。ぼくらが話したのは、自分のいちばん好きなドクター・フーは誰か、いちばん怖い敵はどれか、最高のアシスタントは誰か（ドクター・フーにはいつもアシスタントがいる。たいていイギリス人の女性だ）……といったことだ。

　ドクター・フーは不死身だが、ときに「再生」することがある。再生のためには新しい俳優が必要で、ドクター役はこれまで11人が演じている（いま12人目の時代に入った）。それぞれの俳優がこの役に微妙に違った色を加えていて、たいていのイギリス人にはそれぞれお気に入りのドクターがいる。おそらくイギリスの男性は、いちばん

好きなジェームズ・ボンド役より、いちばん好きなドクター・フー役は誰かを議論することのほうが多いだろう。
　『ドクター・フー』が放映されなかった時代も長かった。80年代に視聴率が落ちたために、1989〜2005年にテレビでの新しいエピソードは作られなかった。復活したときは大変な興奮をもって迎えられ、どうしてこんなに時間がかかったのかと多くの人がいぶかしんだ。『ドクター・フー』という作品は、本当にすばらしい。テーマ音楽は衝撃的だし、ダーレクやサイバーマンといったモンスターはゴジラやキング・コングに劣らないほど印象的だ。おまけにドクター・フーには、これまで発明されたなかで最高の性能を持つ移動装置がある。「ターディス」だ。この不思議な装置は時空を飛び越えるだけでなく、内側は大きいのに外見は電話ボックスほどしかない。そのとおりターディスの外見は、イギリスにあった警察通報用の電話ボックスになっている。最初のシリーズが始まったころには、うまい偽装の方法だった。
　ぼくはもう『ドクター・フー』を毎週は見ていないが、たまに懐かしさから見ることがある。でも白状してしまうと、ぼくの見る回が新しいドクターが最初に登場するときにあたっているのは偶然ではない。ドクター・フーはぼくの子ども時代の一部というだけでなく、この国の生きた象徴のようなものだ。だからイギリス人のひとりとして、ドク

ター・フーを演じるという仕事がきちんと受け継がれているのか確認したくなるのだ。

プロフィール

　コリン・ジョイスは1970年、イギリスでも文化の香りが乏しいエセックス州で生まれる。オックスフォード大学で古代史と近代史を学んだのち、外国語を勉強しようと決意する。不幸なことに日本語を選んでしまい、文法が英語とはまったく異なり、単語も覚えにくいことを知って驚嘆する。

　学生として神戸に住み、その後、浦和と東京に合わせて15年近く住む。これほど長く日本に住んだのは、道を尋ねる以上のことを日本語で言えるようになりたかったためでもあるし、日本での暮らしが楽しかったためでもあるし、そろそろ帰ろうかと思うたびに面白い仕事の話が舞い込んできたためでもある。

　県立高校で英語教員の仕事（あまりいい先生ではなかった）をしたのち、週刊誌『ニューズウィーク日本版』で編集者・記者として働き、その後イギリスで最も読まれている高級紙『デイリー・テレグラフ』の東京特派員となる。

　2007年にニューヨークへ渡り、3年間住む。その間、ブルックリンにほれ込み、アメリカの地ビールが好きになり、英語のアメリカっぽい表現の一部がとても嫌いになる。

　これまで3つの国での経験をもとにした著作がいくつ

かある。そのうち3作は英語で出版されている。*How to Japan*、*An Englishman in N.Y.*、*Let's England* だ。

今はエセックス州のコルチェスターに住む。コルチェスターはロンドン以外にイギリスの首都になったことがある唯一の場所だ。ただし不幸なことに、コルチェスターの短い全盛期は約2000年前にローマ人の支配の下にもたらされたものだが。

現在はフリーランスのジャーナリスト・作家として活動している。エセックス州で最も才能ある書き手のひとりだが、エセックスでの競争がそれほど激しいわけではない。

訳者プロフィール

森田浩之（もりた・ひろゆき）

ジャーナリスト、編集者。『ニューズウィーク日本版』副編集長などを経てフリーランスに。立教大学兼任講師（メディア・スタディーズ）。早稲田大学政治経済学部卒。ロンドン・スクール・オブ・エコノミクス（LSE）メディア学修士。主な訳書にコリン・ジョイス『「イギリス社会」入門』『驚きの英国史』（以上、NHK出版新書）、アリアナ・ハフィントン『誰が中流を殺すのか』（阪急コミュニケーションズ）。著書に『メディアスポーツ解体』（NHKブックス）、『スポーツニュースは恐い』（生活人新書）など。

装丁・本文デザイン	畑中 猛
カバー写真	© Derek James Seaward / Corbis / amanaimages
本文写真	Colin Joyce
校正	大塚葉子
DTP	ドルフィン

本書はNHK『ラジオ英会話』2012年4月号〜2014年3月号のテキストに連載されたエッセイの中から抜粋して加筆・訂正し、日本語訳を付したものです。

LONDON CALLING
Thoughts on England, the English and Englishness

2014（平成26）年6月15日　第1刷発行

著者　　　コリン・ジョイス
訳者　　　森田浩之
　　　　　©2014 Colin Joyce & Hiroyuki Morita
発行者　　溝口明秀
発行所　　NHK出版
　　　　　〒150-8081　東京都渋谷区宇田川町41-1
　　　　　TEL　0570-002-046（編集）
　　　　　TEL　0570-000-321（注文）
　　　　　ホームページ　http://www.nhk-book.co.jp
　　　　　振替　00110-1-49701
印刷・製本　光邦

乱丁・落丁本はお取り替えいたします。
定価はカバーに表示してあります。
Ⓡ＜日本複写権センター委託出版物＞
本書の無断複写（コピー）は、著作権法上の例外を除き、
著作権侵害となります。

Printed in Japan
ISBN 978-4-14-035125-3 C0082